*Frowardness is in his heart, he deviseth
mischief continually; he soweth discord.*

*Therefore shall his calamity come suddenly;
suddenly shall he be broken without
remedy.*

*These six things doth the Lord hate: yea,
seven are an abomination unto him:*

*A proud look, a lying tongue, and hands
that shed innocent blood,*

*An heart that deviseth wicked
imaginations, feet that be swift in running
to mischief,*

*A false witness that speaketh lies, and he
that soweth discord among brethren.*

(Proverbs 6:14-19)

LOST

NATION

LOST NATION

Bobby E. Mills, Ph.D.

Lost Nation

by Bobby E. Mills, Ph.D.

© Copyright 2018

SAINT PAUL PRESS, DALLAS, TEXAS

First Printing, 2018.

ISBN: 9781791672102

Printed in the U.S.A.

Contents

Acknowledgments

Donald J. Trump said that if he were to seek the U.S. Presidency, he would do so as a Republican because "they are the dumbest voters in American society" (People Magazine, 1998). My, oh my, did he ever prove his point! With a little love and email-hijacking from Russia, coupled with a "dab" of assistance from former FBI Director Comey, but more importantly, since 1964 with the hijacking of the Republican Party by Southern Dixiecrats, the Grand Ole Party has been marching in lock step toward "White Privilege" oriented Southern Dixiecrat policies.

The 2016 Presidential election has proven itself to be the most consequential watershed election in the modern era. Most Americans never thought that there would be days like the ones we have witnessed since January 20th, 2017. Without a doubt, American society is spiritually/morally upside-down, because Donald J. Trump is a horrible nightmare for most Americans. Yet, for a select few loyal supporters, he is America's "White Privilege Savior" who vehemently embraced the coded message of "Make America Great (White) Again." To be sure, America's greatness was never enshrined in her white majority population, but in the spiritual-sacred-words enshrined in the Preamble to the U. S. Constitution: "We hold these

Truths to be self-evident, that all Men are created equal, that they are endowed by their Creator with certain unalienable Rights, that among these are Life, Liberty, and the Pursuit of Happiness . . ." Former Governor Jeb Bush prophetically warned America that Donald J. Trump was the "Chaos Candidate" and that he would be a "Chaos President," and he did not exaggerate the point.

I thank my family and endearing friends for their loving support; especially my wife Larnita, my son Daryl Anthony; and my daughters Kelly Leigh and Karen Rene`. Grateful appreciation and heartfelt thanks are extended to Dr. Etta F. Walker and Charles W. Moore for our friendship and stimulating spiritual and intellectual conversations. Finally, thanks to Pastor, Dr. Robert E. Childress, Pastor Raymond L. Farley, Pastor Kelly G. Reynolds, Pastor John E. Cameron, Pastor James Young, and Pastor Paul Smith for spiritually-rewarding conversations over the years.

I love and thank you all, and above all, God's choice blessings to you and yours.

Introduction

The U.S. Constitution is almost a perfectly written political governing document. Yet, Donald J. Trump's ascension to the U.S. Presidency has clearly revealed that socio-psychological screening tests might be necessary tools in order to secure a "More Perfect Union." Most assuredly, America cannot afford the Presidential leadership luxury of another Donald J. Trump-style ungodly mentality in The White House. The election of Donald J. Trump was an incredibly horrible governance mistake. Donald J. Trump declared that he would drain the "swamp" (political-corruption), and yet, he has transformed The White House into a swamp. In fact, President Trump upon taking-up residency in The White House publicly called it a "physical dump," and if you call a place a dump, spiritually and mentally you will treat it as such!

Of course, Trump views The White House as a physical dump, because he does not understand its spiritual meaning in terms of world leadership. Nor does Trump have any spiritual appreciation for the historic artifacts that adorn the facility. Therefore, it goes without saying, Trump is an external physical being who lacks spiritual-moral-character (God Conscience). Just a reminder to Christian Right Evangelicals: "For as he thinketh in his heart, so is he: Eat and drink, saith he to thee; but his heart is not with thee" (Proverbs 23:7). There are some political pundits who believe that we can easily overcome the Trump Presidency, but we all know that once the genie is out of the bottle it is, indeed, difficult to put the genie back into the bottle. Hence, once you weaken the spiritual-moral-foundation of democratic institutions, it is indeed difficult to repair them.

This book is a must read for all Americans for the reasons listed below:

Donald J. Trump did not hijack the Republican Party (Grand Ole Party). He simply snatched the false-covering off Christian Right Evangelicals and the Republican Party, and some confused so-called "Trumpsters" who hijacked Donald J. Trump to reestablish and re-institutionalize a slave-oriented-mentality in American culture based upon White Privilege. Hence, this is why Republicans were so hell bent on exercising control over the Supreme Court. A former Federal Judge, Roy Moore of Alabama said it best: "America was great when slavery existed."

American society must find creative programmatic ways to introduce all Americans to twenty-first century technological advances in order to maximize job creation and work productivity.

Race matters and is still a culturally defining feature of American society. More importantly, God hates racism (Numbers 12:1-16). Unfortunately, President Trump's leadership mentality style of "Alternative-Facts-Confusion" is stoking and rekindling the historic under-current flames of racism in American culture. No doubt about it: you are what you attract. "For God is not the author of confusion, but of peace, as in all churches of the saints" (1 Corinthians 14:33).

Arbitrary societal violence initiated by either civilians or policemen is not an answer to social conflicts and disorganization, but rather causes societal upheaval, and of course, neither are guns and the purchasing of more guns are the answer. This is why Jesus said: "Put up again thy sword into his place: for all they that take the sword shall perish with the sword" (Matthew 26:52). Throughout America's history police constabularies were instituted to protect white males and their property. Even white women were considered property. After the Civil War, the Emancipation Proclamation was enacted on January 1st 1863. At the same time policemen enacted an unwritten "Blue-Code" against Blacks and other minorities in order to maintain the master-slave-relationship. Even after the enactment of laws to protect the Civil Rights of Blacks and other minorities the "Blue-Code" is still alive and well in American society. Unfortunately, in the twenty-first century there is a mentality among some policemen: "Shoot-first, then establish a scenario in your mind why I had to shoot to kill, and then investigate later as a means to justify the death." Kill or be killed. Thus, radicalized individuals who kill because of their belief systems and their god are a serious societal problem.

Family is the universal foundation of every society, and when the family structure as defined and designed by God is altered societies spiritually and morally decline. This is why God has family on His mind. Joshua said it best: "And if it seem evil unto you to serve the Lord, choose you this day whom ye will serve; whether the gods which your fathers served that were on the other side of the flood, or the gods of the Amorities, in whose land ye dwell: but as for me and my house, we will serve the Lord" (Joshua 24:15).

President Trump with bold-faced-lying is tearing down the spiritual-moral-walls of America's democratic institutional structure and civilized human interaction. In fact, Trump's presidential leadership style is internally dividing American against American by attempting to make a "Free Fair Press" the enemy of the people. Hence, there is no such animal as "objective" empirically verifiable truth. Thus, President Trump is transforming international friendships and time-honored allies into enemies, and at the same time, America's enemies into Donald Trump's personal comrades of (PMS): Power, Money, and Sex. Public-political-servant leaders who tell bold-faced lies and create enemies domestic as well as foreign are truly the enemy of the people, not a free press. For after all, the truth unites and a lie divides.

Jesus states it in this spiritually emphatic manner: "If ye continue in my word, then ye are my disciples indeed; and ye shall know the truth, and the truth shall make you free" (John 8:31-32). Unfortunately, Donald J. Trump has enslaved himself to the "art of lying" with the art of a personalized Trump deal and an "American-dumping". But, more importantly, in an ungodly, bold-faced manner, Trump is seeking to further confuse individuals who are already morally and spiritually confused about the true spiritual meaning of life. Of course, these individuals are already seeking justification for their short-comings and moral failures, and therefore, they become "white-privilege-oriented". In other words, they are seeking a free lunch, because they are morally and spiritually challenged and will easily accept lies as truths and truths as lies. For after all, individuals who seek to honor themselves by consistently lying, grabbing for power/money, and creating alternative facts, dishonor themselves because they do not realize that: "The fear of the Lord is the instruction of wisdom; and before honour is humility" (Proverbs 15:33).

Christian Right Evangelicals, the Republican Party (RNC), and Trump

Loyalists, please allow me to remind you: "Righteousness exalteth a nation: but sin is a reproach to any people" (Proverbs 14:34). The love of power and money is the root of all evil. This is what every American should clearly understand: "Submit yourselves therefore to God. Resist the devil, and he will flee from you. Draw nigh to God, and he will draw nigh to you. Cleanse your hands, ye sinners; and purify your hearts, ye double minded" (James 4:7-8). Schisms divide and the truth unites because a schism is an "ism": Racism, Sexism, Classism and so on! However, there is one absolute Biblical equalizing truth that every individual can embrace: "And as it is appointed unto men once to die, but after this the judgment" (Hebrews 9:27).

It is the author's desire that the readers of this book, because of his academic training in the disciplines of Theology (B.D.) as well as Sociology (PhD), that all readers will clearly understand why America is in spiritual-moral-decline. Hence America, in the words of Rodney King, after a severe undeserved-brutal police beating during the L. A. Watts Riots, stated these eloquent words of spiritual inspiration: "Can't we all just get along." Rodney King's words of biblical inspiration are as spiritually profound as it can get. Selah!

A Good Name

"A good name is rather to be chosen than great riches, and loving favour rather than silver and gold" (Proverbs 22:1). What's in a name? The answer is everything, including intellectual integrity and moral character. Thus, a name (reputation) is all that any individual can take out of the world while material riches must be left behind for relatives, friends, thieves, and robbers. Ask the Egyptian Pharaohs if you do not believe me. A rose by any other name is still a rose and smells just as sweet by any other name. In everyday human interactions/relationships, an individual's name is his or her reputation, integrity, and character. A name defines an individual's very existence from whether or not he or she is a person of valor/integrity or one of ill repute who cannot be trusted.

"Neither is there salvation in any other: for there is none other name under heaven given among men, whereby we must be saved" (Acts 4:12). What's in a name? Need I remind you that in the name Jesus there is: Salvation and the opportunity to become a born-again

Christian? Of course, some names are rightfully "Gone with the Wind", because their names have been written on the whirlwind and are now reaping chaos and confusion in time, on time, and all the time. Undoubtedly, some individuals have made a profession of lying, perpetuating racism, sexism, religious bigotry, breaking-up of families with the destruction of moral family values while, concurrently, destroying democratic institutions and "reaping the whirlwind" of confusion. This is why the name JESUS does for humanity what humanity cannot do for SELF.

"There is therefore now no condemnation to them which are in Christ Jesus, who walk not after the flesh, but after the Spirit. For the law of the Spirit of life in Christ Jesus hath made me free from the law of sin and death. For what the law could not do, in that it was weak through the flesh, God sending his own Son in the likeness of sinful flesh, and for sin, condemned sin in the flesh: that righteousness of the law might be fulfilled in us, who walk not after the flesh, but after the Spirit" (Romans 8:1-4). What's in a name? The name Jesus is the righteous pathway to the Kingdom of God as well as Heaven on earth.

Sadly, President Trump, Christian Right Evangelicals, and the Republican Party are determined that we have hell on earth. There will always be some individuals who will ask the eternal question:

"What must I do to be saved?" but, invariably cannot accept Jesus' answer of spiritual rebirth. One example appears as follows:

> And when he was gone forth into the way, there came one running, and kneeled to him, and asked him, Good Master, what shall I do that I might inherit eternal life?
>
> And Jesus said unto him, Why callest thou me good? There is none good but one, that is, God.
>
> Thou knowest the commandments, Do not commit adultery, Do not kill, Do not steal, Do not bear false witness, Defraud not, Honour thy father and mother.
>
> And he answered and said unto him, Master, all these have I observed from my youth.
>
> Then Jesus beholding him loved him, and said unto him. One thing thou lackest: go thy way, sell whatsoever thou hast, and give to the poor, and thou shalt have treasure in heaven: and come, take up the cross, and follow me.
>
> And he was sad at that saying, and went away grieved: for he had great possessions.
>
> —Mark 10:17-21

What's in a name? The name of Jesus is above all names! The Bible called the one referenced above a rich man without name recognition and of low spiritual-moral character. It is his lack of spiritual-moral character understanding which compelled him to go away sad. This is why Jesus said to the disciples: "How hard is it for them that trust in riches to enter into the Kingdom of God" (Mark 10:24). Thus, the rich man demonstrated by his actions that he only loved money and material possessions. This rich man is just like many individuals in twenty-first century America: "lovers of things; lovers of stuff (money)."

America, know this: "A little that a righteous man hath is better than the riches of many wicked" (Psalm 37:16). This is why some individuals voted for an individual to be President who was a known "lover of money" (things), not a lover of people or America. Moreover, they believed that through White-privilege-oriented policies and edits Trump would give them more than what they already have. "For as he thinketh in his heart, so is he" (Proverbs 23:7). Again, President Trump is a "lover of money" judging by his business practices (four bankruptcies). If you are not convinced by his business approach to life, then you might want to consult with Donald J., Jr. (Reference: Vanity Fair Magazine Article: September 1990).

Every individual's greatest need is for love because love calls us into being. God knew us before we were conceived in our mother's womb, even to the number of hairs on each head. Hence, every individual should pray without ceasing that his or her name is written in the Book of Life. Glory hallelujah to the Lamb of God that takes away the sins of the world! What's in a name? God's divine love! "But God commendeth his love toward us, in that, while we were yet sinners, Christ died for us" (Romans 5:8). God is a jealous God and He will have no other gods before him: "For I the Lord thy God am a jealous God, visiting the iniquity of the fathers upon the children unto the third and fourth generation of them that hate me; and shewing mercy unto thousands of them that love me, and keep my commandments" (Exodus 20:5-6). Take heed, Christian Right Evangelicals, Republican Party, and loyal Donald J. Trump supporters who serve President Trump as though he is god, and beware: "Take heed, and beware of covetousness: for a man's life consisteth not in the abundance of the things which he possesseth" (Luke 12:15).

Once again, America, the question is: "What's in a name?" A good name is far better to have than white privilege or silver and gold (money). "No man can serve two masters: for either he will hate the one, and love the other; or else he will hold to the one, and despise the other. Ye cannot serve God and mammon" (Matthew 6:24).

Once again, what's in a name? JESUS, the Good Shepherd. Christian Right Evangelicals, listen up! "Fools make a mock at sin: but among the righteous there is favour" (Proverbs 14:9). Without a doubt, "The steps of a good man are ordered by the Lord: and he delighteth in his way" (Psalm 37:23).

What's in a name? The rich man came to the right Man (Jesus), and he asked the right question. Moreover, he received the right answer but it was not the right answer for him in his heart and mind, and therefore, he went away sad. He could not give it up! This is why "… it is easier for a camel to go through the eye of a needle, than for a rich man to enter the Kingdom of God" (Matthew 19:24).

What's in a name? Salvation for an individual's most precious possession: His SOUL! "How shall we escape, if we neglect so great salvation; which at the first began to be spoken by the Lord, and was confirmed unto us by them that heard him; God also bearing them witness, both with signs and wonders, and with divers miracles, and gifts of the Holy Ghost, according to Christ as a human being" (Hebrews 2:3-4).

What's in a name? Jesus. Jesus Christ. Selah!

The Judas Goat: the Forty-Fifth President

A Judas Goat is an individual who leads sheep (other individuals) to their demise, that is, the slaughter house. Historically, Judas Iscariot is known as the betrayer (son of prediction) of Jesus Christ, the Righteous One, with a kiss and thirty pieces of silver. This is what gives this goat his name. "And while he yet spake, lo, Judas, one of the twelve, came, and with him a great multitude with swords and staves, from the chief priests and elders of the people. Now he that betrayed him gave them a sign, saying, Whomsoever I shall kiss, that same is he: hold him fast. And forthwith he came to Jesus, and said Hail, master; and kissed him" (Matthew 26:47-49). Judas betrayed a Man without sin, Jesus, for thirty pieces of silver (Matthew 26:14-15).

The aftermath of the Putin Summit has revealed President Trump's obvious weakness to be used as Putin's puppet and a "Judas Goat" against America as well as the free world. Trump betrayed his

Presidential Oath which he swore on the Bible to "defend and protect America from both external and internal enemies," for love of power, money, and sex (PMS). Christian Right Evangelicals, RNC, and Trump Loyalists betrayed America at the ballot box, and they did it all in the name of "Re-institutionalizing and Fomenting White Privilege." Shame! Shame! Shame! All of this spiritual-socio-economic confusion in American society has been created behind thirty-six percent of the population following the leadership mentality of a spiritually-confused soul: Donald J. Trump.

Without a doubt, Vladimir Putin has proven through evil actions on the world's stage that he is America's enemy as well as an enemy of the Western Alliance, and above all, the free-world: "Take heed, and beware of covetousness: for a man's life consisteth not in the abundance of the things which he possesseth" (Luke 12:15). President Trump is absolutely correct when he says, "Putin is not my enemy." But Putin is definitely America's enemy, and soon and very soon special prosecutor Mueller will tell the American people whether or not Donald J. Trump is America's enemy; hence, given the private closed-door, two-hour meeting in Helsinki between Putin and President Trump. There is a dead-skunk-on-the-line. Moreover, we have incontrovertible evidence that President Trump is his own worst enemy because of his perpetual, consistent, unadulterated lying. President Trump lies just for the sake of lying because of his morally-flawed character. Presidential lying in and of itself is disgraceful and dishonorable to the men and women who shed blood, and some have even given their lives in the defense of freedom and democratic governance.

President Trump has proven himself to be a lover of money, power, and privilege, because he dishonored the faith of the country, not the flag. Since occupying the Presidential Office, it has been calculated that Trump has made approximately one billion dollars. Is this the real reason he wanted to become President? Just maybe this is why upon taking residence in the White House he called it a dump. This statement in and of itself makes it obvious to reasonable minds that POTUS #45 does not understand the spiritual meaning of The White House as the symbol of freedom and justice for all humanity regardless of national origin. This is precisely why the Bible emphatically declares "For the love of money is the root of all evil: which while some coveted after, they have erred from the faith, and pierced themselves through with many sorrows" (1 Timothy 6:10). Listed below are fact check realities:

1. Four bankruptcies due to financial over-reach.

2. Read: Donald J. Trump, Jr's statement in the September 1990 issue of Vanity Fair Magazine.

3. "No President in history has imposed larger personal

life-style costs on the taxpayers than Donald J. Trump" (David Frum, Senior Editor @ The Atlantic: August 21st 2017 in a tweet).

4. Numerous lawsuits for default on contractual commitments made and the classic example: Trump University settled out of court for 25 million dollars. And, of course, let's not forget the Stormy Daniels lawsuit.

5. The Trump family foundation "shell-game" that is utilizing charitable donations for personal wealth enrichment. For example: commissioning a $20,000 portrait of one's self for self-glorification and paying for it with donated charitable foundation funds.

6. The Billy Bush Access Hollywood Video recording that reveals the lack of spiritual-moral respect that President Trump has for women: mothers, wives, and daughters!

There are many, many more spiritual-moral flaws that could be recounted, but the point is profoundly established: President Trump is by far the most flawed man to ever occupy The White House; hence, to understand this is to spiritually know: "For as he thinketh in his heart, so is he: Eat and drink, saith he to thee; but his heart is not with thee" (Proverbs 23:7). When politicians (RNC) and Party loyalists place the self-centered interests of their political party above the spiritual governing ideals of the country that nation is in deep spiritual trouble. "For where envying and strife is, there is confusion and every evil work. But the wisdom that is from above is first pure, then peaceable, gentle, and easy to be entreated, full of mercy and good fruits, without partially, and without hypocrisy. And the fruit of righteousness is sown in peace of them that make peace" (James 3:16-18).

President Trump is a strife-maker, and Christian Right Evangelicals, Republican Party, as well as, followers of President Trump have become co-conspirators in this spiritual-moral confusion. Without a doubt, "God is not the author of confusion, but of peace, as in all churches of the saints" (1 Corinthians 14:33). There are many spiritually naïve Christian Right Evangelicals, RNC Officials, and Trump Supporters who believe that when Trump is no longer President things will return to some semblance of sanity. Not so, my fellow Americans. Once the genie is out of the bottle, writing philosophically, it is extremely difficult to get him back in that reestablish moral order and democratic civility.

The Republican Party has forgotten what the role of government is all about. This is why they are allowing a spiritually dysfunctional president to cultivate a spirit of division/fear in American society as well as among America's trusted allies (NATO). Christian Right Evangelicals: "Write the vision, and make it plain upon tables. . . For the vision is yet for an appointed time, but at the end it shall speak, and not lie: though it tarry, wait for it; because it will surely come, it will not tarry" (Habakkuk 2:2-3). God is a just God, and that is a fact and not a phenomenon: "Be not deceived: God is not mocked: for whatsoever a man soweth, that shall he also reap. For he that soweth to his flesh shall of his flesh reap corruption; but he that soweth to the Spirit shall of the Spirit reap life everlasting life" (Galatians 6:6-7). Selah!

The Presidential Age Of Alternative Facts

This writer's professional educational training is grounded in both theology and sociology at the Colgate Rochester Crozer Divinity School and Syracuse University. The objectives of my editorial writings in The Forward Times Newspaper are twofold: (a) Any comprehensive sociological perspective about society, social institutions, and human relationships have their intellectual foundation grounded in theological concepts and constructs; (b) theology is about facts and that is the reality of God.

For the wrath of God is revealed from heaven against all ungodliness and unrighteousness of men, who hold the truth in unrighteousness;

Because that which may be known of God is manifest in them; for God hath shown it unto them.

For the invisible things of him from the creation of the

world are clearly seen, being understood by the things that are made, even his eternal power and Godhead; so they are without excuse:

Because that, when they knew God, they glorified him not as God, neither were thankful; but became vain in their imaginations, and their foolish heart was darkened.

Professing themselves to be wise, they became fools,

And changed the glory of the uncorruptible God into an image made like to corruptible man, and to birds, and fourfooted beasts, and creeping things.

—Romans 1:18-23

Sin transforms human beings into animals without soul consciousness of God.

Sociology is about family, society, institutional arrangements as well as interpersonal relationships. This is precisely why my editorial writings have a Biblical/Scriptural foundation, because all of the categories of human understanding are recorded in the Bible, that is, Time, Class, Space, and Number. God's divine ways are not human ways. "For as the heavens are higher than the earth, so are my ways higher than your ways, and my thoughts than your thoughts" (Isaiah 55:9).

The politically-coined phrase "alternative facts" are lies that shallow-minded politicians contrive as attempts to circumvent reality. The truth is the truth, not the truth as an individual desires the truth to be. "These six things doth the Lord hate: yea seven are an abomination unto him: A proud look, a lying tongue, and hands that shed innocent blood, An heart that deviseth wicked imaginations, feet that be swift in running to mischief, A false witness that speaketh lies, and he that soweth discord among the brethren" (Proverbs 6:16-19). Does this remind you of someone you know?

The Republican Party primary process commenced with seventeen individuals, and one by one, they were eliminated; they were decimated by chronic habitual lying. Lies may win for a little while, but in the end TRUTH shall prevail. "Then said Jesus to those Jews which believed on him, if ye continue in my word, then are ye my disciples indeed: and ye shall know the truth, and the truth shall make you free" (John 8:32). The truth does not need any help, and when an individual walks and talks in the truth trouble will show-up.

Without a doubt, all faithful Christians truly know that God has the last word. All Americans must learn to accept social facts as we know them to be, and at the same time work toward positive changes, not negative reactions. Unfortunately, many of the individuals who were victims of bold-faced lies in the Republican Party primary process are now seeking honorific benefits from the perpetrator. Most of these men and one woman must be political party loyalists of low self-esteem and questionable spiritual-moral character. It has rightly been said that power corrupts, and absolute power corrupts absolutely. For after all, the love of power and money are a deadly combination: "For what shall it profit a man, if he shall gain the whole world, and lose his own soul? Or what shall a man give in exchange for his soul?" (Mark 8:36-37). Is it alternative facts (lies)? Seemingly, President Trump only believes in himself, not God, because only he can fix what is wrong in his narrow-minded opinion of American society.

In no unequivocal manner there must be organized political efforts on both sides of the isle as a spiritual, faithful, loyal opposition to bold-faced lying by a presidential administration utilizing alternative facts. "And whatsoever ye do, do it heartily, as to the Lord, and not unto men; knowing that of the Lord ye shall receive the reward of the inheritance: for ye serve the Lord Christ. But he that doeth wrong shall receive for the wrong which he hath done: and there is no respect of persons" (Colossians 3:23-24). It's not about the Party, but the TRUTH of GOD.

In God's sight, equal is equal and not more or less equal. It's not about the PARTY, but what is in the best interests of America, and above all, every citizen and every family. It appears that President Trump is only interested in himself and his family, and America and the rest of the world can go to hell in a hand basket. God has blessed America, and America is a CITY set on a hill for the world to see that what is ultimately good for America is also good for the rest of the world.

Can we truthfully say this is the case with President Trump? The answer is a resounding "HELL NO!" But, he must be held accountable by a free-press and godly legislators who have the best interest of America at heart. God blessed America before President Trump's parents came to America, and has blessed him in spite of his greed for power and money, habitual lying, disrespect for women and minorities, and religious bigotry. Although President Trump has lived in New York City all of his life, it should be clear to all why President Trump probably has never really understood these profound spiritual words inscribed on the Statute of Liberty: "Give me your tired, your poor, your huddled masses yearning to breathe free." President Trump wants to and probably will subliminally replace these sacred spiritual words with "Let's Build That Wall." Walls can make good neighbors, and walls can make bad neighbors on both sides of the wall. Shallow-minded politicians and alternative facts have moral consequences, and the consequences will show up at the most inopportune time.

President Trump's administrative team as well as Cabinet level appointees must spiritually understand that they do not work for President Trump, but they work for and on behalf of the American people, while on the other hand, they must work with the President as an effective administrative team on behalf of the American people because there is not an "I" in the spelling of the concept team. The human "I" as we know it to be, is smack-dab in the middle of sIn. God is the only self-sufficient "I" in the universe. Selah!

Is America For Sale?

The Founders of America's democratic Constitutional system envisioned a system of checks and balances. The election of Donald J. Trump propelled by Christian Right Evangelicals and the complicity of The Republican Party is on the verge of creating a monumental Constitutional crisis (showdown). Christian Right Evangelicals claim to have God-fearing qualities, yet, they elected the most ungodly individual to have ever occupied The White House (Oval Office). Self-righteous Republicans who profess a family-values orientation toward life as well as a Party that places loyalty to an individual rather than country clearly demonstrates in both word and deed that their love is for power and money, not democratic governance. When a major political party allows an ungodly President to openly violate the emolument clause, they then allow America to be placed on the auction block to the highest bidders. Moreover, it appears as though Russia, China, Saudi Arabia, and Israel are the winning bidders, and America is clearly the loser.

No doubt about it, these are spiritually, morally, and socially troubling times for America's democratic institutions. Divisions in American society were not created by President Trump, but his presidential ungodliness has compounded the divisions. Under his immoral presidential leadership, American society has been turned upside down and placed on the auction block (influence, power, sex, and money) to the highest bidders. Shame! Shame! Shame! This is how great nation states begin the process of self-annihilation by intellectually and morally deadening their spiritual senses to immorality for the love of money and power. "Whereby are given unto us exceeding great and precious promises: that by these ye might be partakers of the divine nature, having escaped the corruption that is in the world through lust" (2 Peter 1:4). The Constitutional Founders gave America the Biblical/Spiritual road-map on how not to destroy each other because of the greed factor. The Bible gives us the spiritual road-map to God's spiritual Heaven (life eternally) and on how to achieve "Heaven on earth" that we might escape the corruption of the material world.

America, let's pray that if we survive the dysfunctionality of the Trump Administration, never again shall we vote into the Office of the Presidency an immoral, ungodly, disrespectful, dictatorial-minded demagogue. When the Trump Administration finally exits The White House, we must immediately dispatch Prayer Warriors to the People's House, as Ghost Busters cannot get the job done, because evil spirits (demons) have claimed the territory! If the story of the Prophet Hosea and his marriage to a prostitute (Gomer), one of the oldest professions known to humankind, looks like and sounds like what is taking place in the Trump Administration then, spiritually, you are probably right in your thinking.

Christian Right Evangelicals and The Republican Party elected to the Office of the Presidency the most well-known POLITICAL PIMP of modern times, and they knew it, because Donald J. Trump told the world who he was, what he was, and why he was greater than the most well-known social pimp America has ever known: Iceberg Slim! (I and I alone can fix-it!) Donald J. Trump has not learned that God is the FIXER, and He has proclaimed that which is required of everyone: "He hath shewed thee, O man, what is good; and what doth the Lord require of thee, but to do justly, and love mercy, and to walk humbly with thy God?" (Micah 6:8). Of course, President Trump, Christian Right Evangelicals as well as The Republican Party appear to not have learned this Sunday School lesson at all!

On one particular rainy evening in New York City, the Pimp, Iceberg Slim, observed one of his prostitutes standing under a shelter out of the rain. He rolled down his window and yelled, "Why are you standing rather than working?" The prostitute said, "Iceberg, it is raining!" Iceberg replied, "Walk between the rain-drops because my money better be the same." (Playing God and at the same time imitating the devil). Similarly, President Trump has used his family and network of so-called friends to cut deals and make money off of being President.

Herein lies the long and the short of it all: Is America for sale to the highest bidder(s)? Hosea was one of God's cherished Prophets. God personally permitted him to marry a prostitute whom he faithfully loved that he might personally experience how God feels concerning Israel's unfaithfulness to Him. This is how we allow the devil in others to play tricks with our minds about power and the things of this world. In twenty-first century America, there is a lot of whoredom (spiritual prostitution) going on behind selfish vanity and hoarding. Too many Americans are not looking back and reaching back, because we continually reject the notion that "I am my brother's keeper"; therefore, the rich get richer, and the poor get poorer.

Selfishness and political party corruption for power and the love of money propelled a self-centered demagogue into The White House (the highest Office in the world) based upon an expectation of publicly revitalizing the notion of white privilege. Just as there is no hope in dope, likewise, there is no salvation for America in the leadership mentality of Donald J. Trump, only negative, disastrous consequences for America's democratic institutions as well as America's moral standing in the world community. We are saved by HOPE, not dope. "For we are saved by hope: but hope that is seen is not hope; for what a man seeth, why doth he yet hope for? But if we hope for that we see not, then do we with patience wait for it" (Romans 8:24-25).

It appears as though the powerful nations of the world community are all receiving benefits from the Presidency of Donald J. Trump, and, of course, they saw him coming. Moreover, they all knew that America was for sale. Forewarned is foretold: Family, friends, and business (Power, Money, and Sex) do not mix! Shame! Shame! Shame! America, get right with God, and then we can live in peace and harmony with each other because "All scripture is given by inspiration of God, and is profitable for doctrine, for reproof, for correction, for instruction in righteousness: that the man of God may be perfect, thoroughly furnished unto all good works" (2 Timothy 3:16-17). America, never again blink and elect an ungodly individual to the Office of President. "Be sober, be vigilant; because your adversary the devil, as a roaring lion, walketh about seeking whom he may devour: whom resist steadfast in the faith, knowing that the same afflictions are accomplished in your brethren that are in the world" (1 Peter 5:8-9). Selah!

"Gone With The Wind"

"Gone with the wind" are the days when America was great. Of course, Native American Indians knew that North America was great prior to the Pilgrims landing at Plymouth Rock. They only took from the land that which was necessary to sustain life because they understood that nature was not an endless, plentiful resource. There is a time to plant and a time to harvest; moreover, "To everything there is a season, and a time to every purpose under the heaven" (Ecclesiastes 3:1). America, "Take heed, and beware of covetousness: for a man's life consisteth not in the abundance of the things which he possesseth" (Luke 12:15). Hence, most things that are worthwhile and eternal cannot be achieved utilizing the barrel of guns. This is why Jesus Christ, the Righteous One, warned Peter about the wisdom of not using the sword (guns) (Matthew 26:52).

Alabama Republican Senatorial Candidate, Judge Roy Moore, emphatically declared that the last time America was great was during slavery. Know full well, America, chattel slavery has truly

"Gone with the Wind." However, there are still some residual vestiges of chattel slavery in existence in the twenty-first century, in the minds of some Christian Right Evangelical churches, because they still desire white privilege; that is, something for nothing, and when you desire something for nothing, invariably, you get nothing. And, nothing from nothing leaves nothing. "Professing themselves to be wise, they became fools, And exchanged the glory of the incorruptible God for an image made in the form of corruptible man and of the birds and four footed animals and crawling creatures. Therefore God gave them over in the lusts of their hearts to impurity, that their bodies might be dishonored among them. For they exchanged the truth of God for a lie, and worshiped and served the creature rather than the Creator, who is blessed forever. Amen" (Romans 1:22-25).

This Scriptural verse is referencing spiritual ignorance that is the love of power, money, and sex—all pleasures of the flesh. President Trump has emphatically declared that he will return America to its past greatness by reestablishing a dictatorial white-privilege-oriented, male-dominated culture which existed in all of its vulgarity prior to 1964-1965 (Civil Rights Act and Voting Rights Act). The Trump Campaign Slogan "Make America Great Again," was about white male dominance, and minority and female status subjugation utilizing power, money, and sex as instruments of discrimination.

Without a doubt, America was great in 1776 when the Constitutional Framers had the spiritual-moral courage at the Continental Congress in Philadelphia to write the Preamble to the U.S. Constitution and the Articles of the Constitution, to give moral notice to Great Britain that it was no longer in charge, and its colonial authority was "Gone with the wind." Unfortunately, since that time, America has had a checkered white-privilege-oriented history of human usury. America used or took advantage of Native Americans, African slaves, and other European ethnic immigrants while declaring, behold, look at what we (whites) made out of an undeveloped savage land and the civilization we (white males) carved out of the wilderness. Certainly the abundance of America was present prior to the arrival of whites on these shining shores. The Pilgrims landed at Plymouth Rock and then commenced throwing rocks at every other racial-ethnic group that came to these shining shores by creating a totem-pole-cast class system of white male privilege.

America has a spiritual Presidential leadership crisis of epidemic proportions, not to mention, family breakdown, the opioid addiction crisis, and the spiritual-moral deterioration of civil standards of human decency. The leadership structure (White Males and

Christian Right Evangelicals) are blaming everyone but themselves, and they are in-charge. Moreover, it has become commonplace for Americans to be besieged by mad mass gun violence. Americans, we should spiritually remind ourselves that "Power corrupts, and absolute power corrupts absolutely." Great nations decline and have fallen because of internal spiritual-moral decay.

Corrupt leadership mentalities in high places are always more serious problem. America can handle external physical forces/enemies. Going along to get along to advance personal agendas rather than nation-state building agendas is America's critical problem. Eventually, failed leadership asks this question: What happened? The answer lies in this Scripture because we cease to glorify, honor, and praise God from whom all blessings flow: "Let us therefore come boldly unto the throne of Grace, that we may obtain mercy, and find grace to help in time of need" (Hebrews 4:16). "Gone with the Wind" are the days when God spiritually led America in its time of need. The Trumps of America now lead with the battle-cry: "Money, honey" while singing the money song: "Get the money! Get the money: Any kind of way get the money." Shame! Shame! Shame!

Lest we forget, America's greatness (infrastructure-development) was built by free slave labor, not white land grabbers! Moreover,

Blacks never did receive the reparations promised after the Civil War, but other abused and misused social groups including Native Americans, did receive some reparations for what was taken by the barrel of guns. Since 1964 (starting with Senator Barry Goldwater), the Republican Party has been steadily marching America toward electing a Donald J. Trump dictatorial-style personality as President (The Rebirth of Ole Dixie). In 2016, because of its governing policies, the Republican Party became the de facto Ole Southern Dixiecrat Party of the South. More importantly, with Donald J. Trump as its standard bearer, Republicans sought to replicate the evil-policy traditions of the past rather than embracing America's multi-cultural future.

The evils of the past should never become the future simply because the past was imperfect—not because of God, but because of evil men (the devil). America, be not deceived; behold the truth of God: "Neither is there salvation, in any other: for there is none other name under heaven given among men, whereby we must be saved" (Acts 4:12). By no stretch of anyone's narrow-minded imagination is President Donald J. Trump the male or his name the name by which Americans or America will be saved. Of course, this includes all of his loyal so-called Christian Right Evangelical supporters. Hence, and forevermore, Jesus explicitly came to seek and save those who were lost, and "Neither is there salvation in any other: for there is none other name under heaven given among men, whereby we must be saved" (Acts 4:12). President Donald Trump, Judge Roy Moore, and Mr. Stephen Bannon, gone forever are the days when slavery made America great. Selah!

The Blame Game

Blame, blame, and blame is the name of the President Trump White House Game: Oops! Gang. The Trump administration is unwilling to take responsibility for their own decisions; therefore, Trump and The White House project the blame for their administrative dysfunction upon President Obama, House Minority Leader Nancy Pelosi, Senate Minority Leader Schumer, or the Democratic Party in general. Above all, President Trump is a blame-game specialist. Shame! Shame! Shame!

What is it for The Trump White House to lie? America, remember the story of "Chicken Little" who was always telling people "the sky is falling; the sky is falling." One day Chicken Little went out and the sky was falling, but no one would listen to him. America, understand well, and heed the unadulterated Word of God because Jesus said it best: "Yea rather, blessed are they that hear the word of God, and keep it" (Luke 11:28). God has warned us about individuals such as President Donald J. Trump: "When he speaketh fair, believe him not:

for there are seven abominations in his heart. Whose hatred is covered by deceit, his wickedness shall be shown before the whole congregation (nation/world)" (Proverbs 26:25-26). President Trump is a fake leader with no shame in his political game; only an insatiable desire to blame others for his own failures. Whatever happened to "I and I alone can fix-it"? Tweeting, blaming previous presidential administrations, and ungodly political posturing is not public-policy decision-making.

Christian Right Evangelicals are seemingly more spiritually in tune with sin than the righteousness of God simply because of their overwhelming support for a no-God-conscience individual such as President Donald J. Trump. America, this is indeed a mind-boggling, spiritually-disturbing reality. Saying, "Lord, Lord," and running with the devil is truly an ungodly abomination. The Christian church should never become a country club whereby pastoral leaders espouse spiritual words of inspiration from pulpits that simply fall upon deaf ears in the pews. Now, we know why Sunday morning is the most segregated hour in American society. Shame, shame, because money is the name of the game, and now we know what "In God We Trust" truly means to Christian Right Evangelicals. Christian Right Evangelicals understand this: "For the love of money is the root of all evil: which while some coveted after, they have erred from the faith, and pierced themselves through with many sorrows"

(1 Timothy 6:10). Nevertheless, Christian Right Evangelicals, "God judgeth the righteous, and God is angry with the wicked every day" (Psalm 7:11).

Christians should never support ungodly leadership mentalities such as that of President Trump and his counterpart Russian Dictator Putin, especially with nuclear capacity at their finger-tips. God has declared no more water but fire next time. Moreover, God has given us the privilege of self-governance: the sacred democratic right to vote. And, if individuals do not intelligently know what to vote for, then maybe they should stay home. By the way, not voting is not a godly choice, but it is probably more desirable than placing an ungodly individual in The White House (The People's House).

America has experienced one hundred (100) days of hell because we have a spiritually misguided President who does not understand democratic leadership, but who has an ungodly love for communistic dictatorship. President Trump for the past one hundred (100) days has been acting as though he is stuck-on-hellish-stupidity. As a result, American society has experienced hell and is spiritually upside down without positive solutions to any of its socio-economic problems. American society is in socio-political turmoil. Its democratic institutions are being compromised, and an ungodly war is on the horizon to protect against impending impeachment proceedings for treason. Moreover, making off-the-wall war talk and sword-raddling against an unstable dictatorial regime together produce a recipe for world annihilation. We all know that a war-time President will not be impeached or lose a Presidential election.

America, remember what God told Samuel (Israel's last Judge) to tell the Israelites about their desire for a king and their desire to be like other nations: "And the Lord said unto Samuel, Hearken unto the voice of the people in all that they say unto thee: for they have not rejected thee, but they have rejected me, that I should not reign over them . . . And Samuel heard all of the words of the people, and he rehearsed them in the ears of the Lord. And the Lord said to Samuel, Hearken unto their voice: howbeit yet protest solemnly unto them, and shew them the manner of the King that shall reign over them" (1 Samuel 8:6-9). God warned the Israelites: A king can be compromised; but the Israelites could not compromise the man of God (Samuel). And, of course, Saul was not God's choice for king of the Israelites.

On the 99th day of his Presidency, Donald J. Trump told the world in so many words: "I was qualified to be President (American Citizen), but I was not ready to be President of a great nation, because I did not know the complexity of American social democracy and the amount of complicated-work involved." Once again, whatever happened to: "I and I alone can fix-it"? It's not easy being the President of the greatest nation on the planet.

Unfortunately, the Republican Party has become a nationalistic (White-Privilege-Oriented) grievance party; that is, a Political Party whose voting base is made up of individuals who have socio-economic grievances against our democratic system of government based upon race/ethnicity as "The-Angry-White-Privilege-Right," not The Christian Evangelical Right. Base-line Republican voters are using socio-economic issues simply as a way to mask racism, bigotry, and sexism. The Party of Lincoln is spiritually dead. The Southern Dixiecrat Party and the Party of Reagan is alive and well, but the Party of Lincoln (Grand Ole Party) is dead.

To top it off, we have had disastrous Republican Town Hall Meetings that turned into shouting matches and mayhem, the legislative debacle of repeal and replace Obamacare, building a Mexican-Style Berlin-Style Wall, the General Flynn Treason Investigation, Presidential midnight tweeting, The Trump-style War brigade, and the North Korean Mad-Man-Show. Three more years of this? God help us all. Even though God has already blessed America, too many Americans refuse to bless and honor God! America, we are on the edge of midnight; and God is angry with the wicked everyday as well as with those who seek to perpetuate evil. Thus: "Let us therefore come boldly unto the throne of grace, that we may obtain mercy, and find grace to help in time of need" (Hebrews 4:16). Amen! Amen! Amen!

Supreme God: U.S. Supreme Court

America, be careful what you ask for because you just might receive it. Know full well that "God judgeth the righteous, and God is angry with the wicked every day" (Psalm 7:11). The real Supreme Court is in Heaven whereby every individual is destined to meet face-to-face the Eternal Judge (Supreme God) of all things and be righteously judged spiritually for deeds done in the flesh. "And as it is appointed unto men once to die, but after this the judgment" (Hebrews 9:27). Therefore, "Ye adulterers and adulteresses, know ye not that the friendship of the world is enmity with God? Whosoever therefore will be a friend of the world is the enemy of God. Do ye think that the scripture saith in vain. The spirit that dwelleth in us lusteth to envy? But he giveth more grace unto the humble" (James 4:4-6).

Understanding the carnal-minded personality of the forty-fifth President, it should not surprise anyone that the Trump

Administration had no plan for reunification of immigrant children and their parents. But, they had an evil-sinister plan for breaking up families and adopting out children, because this is what carnal minds do. "For to be carnal minded is death; but to be spiritually minded is life and peace. Because the carnal mind is enmity against God: for it is not subject to the law of God, neither indeed can it be. So then they that are in the flesh cannot please God" (Romans 8:6-8).

The refugee crisis on the southern border was known for months, and the Trump Administration prepared for months on end to deal with the circumstance in an unrighteous and ungodly manner. Americans clearly understand what is wrong with illegal immigration: It is illegal. However, this was not illegal immigration. It was refugees seeking asylum from horrible gang violence and economic mayhem in their home countries in Latin America. Therefore, the refugee problem will continue to exist and even get worse as long as the Trump Administration and America refuse to help Latin America solve its structural socio-economic-political-problems.

America, black lives as well as all other lives matter! God hates racism, and He is no respecter of personalities, wealth, social statuses, or any other arbitrary social designations (Number 12:1-2). Since the Emancipation Proclamation constabularies (Law

Enforcement Agencies) were established to protect Whites especially white men and their property, not the Civil Rights of Blacks and minorities. This was accomplished by any means necessary, including lynching, murder, bullying/intimidating methods, and arbitrary laws and their arbitrary enforcement.

In the twenty-first century these conditions have worsened because Law Enforcement Agencies are now being manned by many military-minded post-traumatic-syndrome-oriented personalities. At the same time, medical professionals are telling us that most military individuals suffer from post-traumatic-syndrome disorder. Socio-psychologically this is what is called a compound-complex problem of social injustice, because now you have potentially unstable personalities with guns and badges: A license to kill Blacks as well as other minorities.

The Trump Administration by seeking to re-institute and legalize White-Privilege-oriented policies is radicalizing religious fanaticism in the name of their god (racism). If America is not prayerful as well as diligent, she is headed for the eternal bonfire (Armageddon). But, know this: "There is one God, and one mediator between God and men, the man Christ Jesus; who gave himself a ransom for all, to be testified in due time" (1 Timothy 2:5-6). Christian Right Evangelicals, the RNC, and Trump Loyalists, President Trump is not the answer to

America's socio-spiritual problems, and you have become a willing part of the problem. Justice is a spiritual concept, and the administration of justice is spiritual as well, for after all, no society can legislate effectively morality, even though America has emphatically declared that we have the sacred "Halls of Justice" and the scales of justice are blind.

But more often than not, for many and varied reasons, justice for some is in the halls and not in the courtroom, because the thumb is always on the scales. God and Jesus the Righteous One knew this about the human spirit since the spiritual fall of Adam and Eve in the Garden of Eden. God gave Adam and Eve one spiritual law: "Don't eat of the tree in the center of the Garden." Yet, human beings because of sin (separation from God) created 613 Hebraic Laws, and the Israelites could not live by their own laws. God condensed the 613 laws to the Ten Commandments with Moses on Mount Sinai and still we are not able to abide by them.

Jesus reduced the Ten Commandments to the Two Great Commandments, and still we have not been able to live by them because of a lack of God-conscience (Spiritual separation from God). Moreover, God-conscience has been replaced with the PMS conscience of vanity: Power, Money, and Sex! The RNC, Christian Right Evangelicals, Trump Loyalists, as well as Trump himself, do not comprehend the following Scripture of inspiration: "Thou wilt keep him in perfect peace, whose mind is stayed on thee: because he trusteth in thee" (Isaiah 26:3). PMS for women is produced by nature and is a natural process of cleansing for potential new birth; however, for men, PMS is an unnatural (sinful) socio-economic condition of VANITY for the love of power, money, and sex.

Unfortunately, the U.S. Supreme Court is often utilized to promulgate extremism the personal vanity of white men (unrighteousness), not justice for all. The RNC, Christian Right Evangelicals, President Trump, and the tenets of White Privilege which is a figment of false imaginations have been cultivated over time. Understand this Conservatives and Liberals: "Professing themselves to be wise, they became fools, and changed the glory of the uncorruptible God into an image like to corruptible man" (Romans 1:22-23). Hence, if both Liberals as well as Conservatives would seek to understand God in a search for the "truth" they would understand universal humanity. Take heed, my brothers and sisters in the fellowship of Christ (Righteousness): "Set your affection on things above, not on things on the earth. For ye are dead, and your life is hid with Christ in God. When Christ, who is our life, shall appear, then shall ye also appear with him in glory" (Colossians 3:2-4).

Beware, Supreme Court Justices, how you interpret the Constitutional Law "equal-justice" under the law because: ". . . as it is appointed unto men once to die, but after this the judgment" (Hebrews 9:27). RNC, Christian Right Evangelicals, and Trump Advisors, please tell this confused soul (President Trump) these words of spiritual inspiration: "Moreover if thy brother (Putin) shall trespass against thee, go and tell him his fault between thee and him alone: if he shall hear thee, thou hast gained thy brother. But if he will not hear thee, then take with thee one or two more, that in the mouth of two or three witnesses every word may be established. And if he shall neglect to hear them, tell it unto the church: but if he neglect to hear the church, let him be unto thee as a heathen man and a publican" (Matthew 18:15-17). Mueller and the FBI know what's going on and what has gone on, because they are working toward an end and not talking. Moreover, they have interview some eye witnesses to all that has gone on. Selah!

Can America Forgive Itself?

Every great nation has spiritual and moral growing pains, and America is not an exception because she still has spiritual developmental pains related to her spiritually-troubled past that continues to plague her even in the twenty-first century. Thus, in our thinking and moral actions, we must strive for national unity. That is, we must always strive for national spiritual-moral interdependence, because "A Nation divided against itself cannot stand." In so doing, there must be social and institutional processes that foster individual/collective spiritual and moral conscience that can be enacted into just social laws. Unfortunately, the overwhelming support of Christian Right Evangelicals for the presidency of Donald J. Trump to represent the sacred and highest office in the world community has brought to the international forefront America's ugly, ungodly deeds of the past: The annihilation of Native Americans and the ungodly, spiritual, inhumanity of slavery.

Historically, America has tried to justify her abominable sins of destroying an entire nation (Native Americans) by claiming to have built a "better more" prosperous civilization. However, it must be stated that Native Americans thought America was a paradise, because they only consumed what they needed. But, the mentality of the first settlers was like unto that of Nero's burning Rome while playing his fiddle and declaring (claiming), he would build a better Rome. Shortly, thereafter, Whites had an internal Civil War, because they could not get along with themselves. Of course, the White versus White power struggle was grounded in the greed factor (economics), and above all, ungodliness.

There were some godly Whites, who knew that slavery was spiritually ungodly, and they resisted the evil of it all, for example John Brown. Thus, because of America's sins of the past, we should clearly understand why we must not repeat the sins of the past. Moreover, Americans even commissioned slave ships to go to the Continent of Africa, the origin and cradle of humanity (civilization), for free labor using the barrel of guns. Do Whites believe that an eternal civilization can be achieved through the barrel of guns or other weaponry? If so, let's just ask Alexander the Great, the Caesars, Gangus Khan, Egyptian Pharaohs, The Kaiser, and Hitler.

Man's evil is buried with his bones. Christian Right Evangelicals take heed and beware: ". . . as it is appointed unto men once to die, but after this the judgment" (Hebrews 9:27).

The election of Donald J. Trump is a clear historically-recorded, moral example in America's political history of how a great nation-state can lose its national conscience; that is, an understanding of right versus wrong. All great nations fall because of internal moral denigration. The love of money and the ungodly quest for power through White Privilege will assure Americans of separation from God as well as unrighteousness. that is, create hell on earth rather than Heaven on earth. "Professing themselves to be wise, they became fools" (Romans 1:22).

Christian Right Evangelicals, in electing "Donald J. Trump" to the sacred office of the Presidency, you fulfilled the spiritual-moral-social meaning as well as reality prophecy of this Scriptural verse: "Fools make a mock at sin: but among the righteous there is favour" (Proverbs 14:9). Moreover, Christian Right Evangelicals, you failed your sacred duty to yourselves, your children, and your children's children. More importantly, you failed the Nation you claim to love by electing an individual who told you in no uncertain terms that he was spiritually and morally bankrupt (troubled-one-very-side). "Let no man deceive you with vain words: for because of these things cometh the wrath of God upon the children of disobedience. Be not therefore partakers with them." (Ephesians 5:6-7). Hence, you lost favor with God because of your spiritual failure to "Trust in the Lord with all thine heart; and lean not unto thine own understanding. In all of thy ways acknowledge him, and he shall direct thy paths" (Proverbs 3:5-6). Shame! Shame! Shame!

"Finally, my brethren, be strong in the Lord, and in the power of his might. Put on the whole armour of God, that ye may be able to stand against the wiles of the devil. For we wrestle not against flesh and blood, but against principalities, against powers, against the rulers of darkness of this world, against spiritual wickedness in high places" (Ephesians 6:10-12). Christian Right Evangelicals, this Scriptural verse, in and of itself, informs every American that the "swamp" is not being drained, but is being maintained, cultivated, and replaced with more ungodly "SWAMP" creatures.

In as much as, "The Lord gave the word: great was the company of those who published it" (Psalm 68:11). Take heed, Christian Right Evangelicals and Republican Party: "Lay hands suddenly on no man, neither be partaker of other men's sins: keep thyself pure" (1 Timothy 5:22). Thus, know this: as Christians in striving to be Christ-like, we should "Come boldly unto the throne of grace, that we may obtain mercy, and find grace to help in time of need" (Hebrews

4:16).

The White House is a sacred place because it is "Of the people, by the people, and for the people." Shortly after becoming president, Donald J. Trump called The White House a "PHYSICAL DUMP"; as soon as he moved into it, The White House became a "SPIRITUAL DUMP" simply because of Trump's toxic, ungodly leadership mentality. Shame! Shame! Shame! Work is the gift of God; and, therefore, when individuals work for things, they create holes in their souls. Work is spiritual self-fulfillment, not materialism. As Americans, we need to stop pretending how we feel about each other because it is not about individual feelings, but God's will as expressed in the Two Great Commandments: "The Lord our God is one Lord: and thou shalt love the Lord thy God with all thy heart, and with all thy soul, and with all thy mind, and with all thy strength: this is the first commandment. And, the second is likewise, namely this, Thou shalt love thy neighbor as thyself" (Mark 12:29-31).

Finally, Christian Right Evangelicals and Republican Party, not man (Donald J. Trump), BUT GOD "Who his own self bare our sins in his own body on the tree, that we, being dead to sins, should live unto righteousness; by whose stripes ye were healed. For ye were as sheep going astray; are now returned unto the Shepherd and Bishop of your souls" (1 Peter 2:24-25). Therefore, do not lose your soul(s) by following after an ungodly man because of your love of things rather than the love of God, which was in Christ Jesus reconciling the world. It is "Come-by-here, Lord" time" in America. "For he saith, I have heard thee in a time accepted, and in the day of salvation have I succoured thee: behold, now is the accepted time; behold, now is the day of salvation" (2 Corinthians 2:2). Shalom (Peace)!

Internal Values Versus External Values

There is an eternal-spiritual question that confronts every human being: Who do you love more, the Creator or the Creation? God is the Creator of all things, and He loves human beings above all things, but God never told us that it would be easy. We messed things up in the Garden of Eden. Yes, "We are troubled on every side, yet not distressed; we are perplexed, but not in despair; persecuted, but not forsaken; cast down, but not destroyed" (2 Corinthians 4:8-9). Therefore, every Christian believer should tell the Good News of the Gospel everywhere: in church houses, whore houses, dope houses, ungodly houses, and (especially) in the Donald J. Trump House, that is, the sacred people's house called The White House.

We must always remember this: "For God so loved the world, that he gave his only begotten Son, that whosoever believeth in him should not perish, but have eternal life" (John 3:16). Every individual's answer to the question at hand will determine his/her quality of spiritual life. Even the quality of family life interaction is determined by an individual's answer to this question. Society begins and ends with family structure; hence, the quality of life of any society is influenced by family-values orientations. The Christian faith spiritually emphasizes the importance of internal family values rather than external materialistic values as recorded in this Scriptural verse: "This is a faithful saying, and worthy of all acceptation, that Christ Jesus came into the world to save sinners; of whom I am chief" (1 Timothy 1:15).

The visible presence of the Word of God (Bible) should always be a part of every family's daily routine because salvation comes through the generation. "This day is salvation come to this house" (Luke 19:9). This is why the life of Jesus begins with the genealogy of Jesus: Generational Connections. Maybe this is why in American society we have two lost generations in the twenty-first century: "Babies having babies." Seeking to maximize the pleasure-principle is a dangerous spiritual-moral proposition because ". . . she that liveth in pleasure is dead while she liveth" (1 Timothy 5:6): This Scriptural verse includes males too! Clearly, "babies birthing babies" in American society has produced a class of dysfunctional parents as well as dysfunctional family structures.

"Thou art worthy O Lord, to receive glory and honor and power: for thou hast created all things, and for thy pleasure they are and were created" (Revelation 4:11). Hence, internal spiritual values foster living from the inside to the outside; thus, an external value system encourages materialism (outside living). When individuals value materialistic things, they can create more so than themselves and each other; that is, they reverse the spiritual order of God based upon the Two Great Commandments. Moreover, when we were growing up as children, responsible parents would not allow children to play outside too long. After playing outside for a while, they would make them come into the house to teach them an important life principle or lesson: Don't stay outside too long, for its dangerous and not good for you.

In twenty-first century America, we have two generations of Americans who were not taught this important spiritual life lesson. They have been playing outside too long! Unfortunately, they think that the acquisition of things can make an individual happy. God desires that individuals work for spiritual self-fulfillment, not to purchase material things. Well, Christian Right Evangelicals, "Take heed, and beware of covetousness: for a man's life consisteth not in the abundance of the things which he possesseth" (Luke 12:15). Without a doubt, if things made individuals happy, America would be the happiest place on planet earth. Of course, every American knows this is not the case, because materialism encourages the "get-more-syndrome," the "need-more-syndrome," and the "got-to-have-more-syndrome." God gave human beings dominion over the earth; therefore, individuals must be taught and must learn how to be good stewards by spiritually being "fruitful, and multiply, and replenish the earth, and subdue it" (Man and Woman). (Genesis 1:28). This can only be achieved by reading and studying God's Word. "Blessed is he that readeth, and they that hear the words of this prophecy, and keep those things which are written therein: for the time is at hand" (Revelation 1:3).

Internal spiritual values help individuals overcome the moral confusion in the world, even though the devil is the prince of the world. Christian Right Evangelicals, this is why a Christian must be in the world but not of the world. Moreover, when a male tells you who he is, and what he is, believe him. You cannot get a clean thing from an unclean thing. Therefore, know this Christian Right Evangelicals: Donald J. Trump has proven himself to be unclean in all things. And, if you do not know this by now, pray, because you have a God problem. Those of you who rationalized voting for President Trump, because he told you he would drain the "SWAMP" and make Washington work for you, now know that Washington is working for the Trump family and Trump cronies. America, know this: a swamp-minded individual cannot and will not drain the swamp because, first and foremost, he must first drain the pollution from his mind by spiritually seeking God. "Sanctify them through thy truth: thy word is truth" (John 17:17). Moreover, individuals should "Study to shew thyself approved unto God, a workman that needeth not be ashamed, rightfully dividing the word of truth" (2 Timothy 2:15).

Democracy and democratic institutions can only be sustained by a society of individuals whose value orientation is INTERNAL rather than external. Thus, a society of individuals whose primary value orientation is external can easily be lulled or mentally and physically forced into accepting communism, fascism, or a dictatorial leadership; hence, by precept and example, we should teach our children, who are our future, what God requires of us because "He hath shewed thee, O man, what is good; and what doth the Lord require of thee, but to do justly, and to love mercy, and to walk humbly with thy God" (Micah 6:8).

The children of Parkland, Florida, should not have to remind us of our sacred duty, obligation, and responsibility to our future. "Lo, children are an heritage of the Lord: and the fruit of the womb is his reward" (Psalm 127:3). Who do you love: guns or children? Obviously, President Trump does not understand, nor is he willing to be taught any spiritual wisdom; therefore, Christian Right Evangelicals, in case you have forgotten, we have an eternal Savior in Heaven who is preparing an eternal place for your soul. His name is Jesus Christ, the Righteous One. You should never forget it, because neither President Trump nor any other mortal man can save the world; only God has the power to do so, and He has already done so through Jesus Christ: "Who his own self bare our sins in his own body on the tree, that we, being dead to sins, should live unto righteousness: by whose stripes ye were healed" (1 Peter 2:24). Selah!

America: What Is It Really About?

In 2008 and 2012, ninety-six percent of Blacks who voted in the Presidential elections voted for Barack Obama; however, they did not vote for President Obama for Black Privilege. Blacks sought societal fairness and social justice for all Americans. Blacks knew that President Obama would be just and fair-minded to all Americans and at the same time be limited in his abilities to remedy past and present inequities leveled against Blacks, and other minorities. On the other hand, this is precisely why Republican leaders in both the Senate and House of Representatives emphatically declared that their objective was to make President Obama a "One-Term President," and furthermore, would politically obstruct his efforts to accomplish anything of substance. The White House is painted white, and is called The White House both for physical, symbolic and real-life-reasons or consequences. This is why the Birther Movement was instituted by Republicans and

Donald J. Trump, in particular. The Birther Movement was simply an ungodly attempt at politically delegitimizing the election of a black man and his family to reside in The White House at 1600 Pennsylvania Avenue.

In the 2016 Presidential election, the majority of Trump voters were not working class. In fact, four out of five Christian Right "White" Evangelicals voted for Donald J. Trump. During the Republican Party Primary, Trump voters were mostly affluent Whites. Forty-two percent of white women voters voted for Trump. Fifty-three percent of white males voted for Trump. Amazingly, for some strange and contestable reason(s), twenty-nine percent of Hispanic voters also voted for Trump. Apparently, Trump-Hispanic voters did not watch, neither did they understand Trump's announcement speech. Or, they must not have understood his psychotic feelings (Nut-Case-Reaction) toward Hispanics and other minorities. America cannot be made White again. The "White Only" signs still remain indelibly in the hearts and minds of some spiritually confused Whites, but we pray and diligently work toward the physical "White Only" signs never returning.

The slogan "Make America Great Again" is an attempt at bringing back the past which, in turn, was not good for Whites, Blacks, or any other cultural minority group. America has always been the greatest nation-state that has ever existed yesterday or today, and all Americans should pray that it remains so. Let's pray that Republican Party Officials do not allow President Trump to destroy our sacred democratic institutions based upon the principle of "In God We Trust." Apparently, too many Republican Loyalists and Christian Right Evangelicals are placing their trust in the "I, and only I can fix it" man (President Donald J. Trump), rather than in Almighty God. America is a multi-cultural society forever and forever, because no individual or nation can turn back the hands of time. Time marches on, because TIME belongs to God! But free-will choices belong to each individual.

What transforms a house into a home? "Love and self-sacrifice". Likewise, what transforms a collection of diverse individuals, families, and different socio-cultural groupings into a cohesive democratic nation-state? And, a just body of Constitutional laws as well as a spiritual understanding of the ultimate meaning of life. "I am my brother's keeper," not my brother's killer. (Reference: The Biblical Cain and Abel story as recorded in the book of Genesis.)

The election of Donald J. Trump has propelled American society into a morally-confused state of internal political chaos, external leadership decline, distrust, and utter disrespect. President Trump's leadership-mentality-style has threatened international (world) moral order. Every ungodly divisive political declaration and devilish promise made by Donald J. Trump during the Republican Party Primary is being institutionalized as a new world order that only he and President Putin will control. Wake up, America, and behold the impending destruction that is nipping and knocking at the very moral fiber of our nation. "For the law of the Spirit of life in Christ Jesus hath made me free from the law of sin and death. For what the law could not do, in that it was weak through the flesh..." (Romans 8:2-3).

As a nation-state, we are all guilty and responsible for the state of our national politics, political party system, as well as the election of President Donald J. Trump. United we stand, divided we fall. We have allowed an ungodly chasm to develop in our society and its democratic institutions, because of the love of power, money, and sex (PMS). "I beseech you therefore, brethren, by the mercies of God, that ye present your bodies a living sacrifice, holy acceptable unto God, which is your reasonable service. And be not conformed to this world: but be ye transformed by the renewing of your mind, that ye may prove what is that good, and acceptable, and perfect, will of God" (Romans 12:1-2).

America, before it is too late, before the eternal lights go out for each individual and the final curtain comes down, know full well:

"And as it is appointed unto men once to die, but after this the judgment" (Hebrews 9:27). Let's remove the foolishness out of our democratic governmental institutions, because "Fools make a mock at sin: but among the righteous there is favor" (Proverbs 14:9). The foundation of foolishness is lying, dealing in illicit monetary transactions, dealing in unnatural pleasures, and having an aught with your fellowman.

America, God is pleading with you in these trying-morally-challenging times to "Be sober, be vigilant; because your adversary the devil, as a roaring lion, walketh about, seeking whom he may devour: whom resist stedfast in the faith, knowing that the same afflictions are accomplished in your brethren that are in the world" (1 Peter 5:8-9). When godly individuals are determined to do well (good), who can stop them? We know "The steps of a good man are ordered by the Lord: and he delighteth in his way. Though he fall, he shall not be utterly cast down: for the Lord upholdeth him with his hand." (Psalm 37: 23-24). Selah!

Ungodly Words Incite Devilish Deadly Actions

"Death and life are in the power of the tongue" (Proverbs 18:21)

It has rightfully been said words matter and often times can have deadly consequences. "In the beginning was the Word, and the Word was with God, and the Word was God. The same was in the beginning with God. All things were made by him; and without him was not anything made that was made" (John 1:1-2). Moreover, "A soft answer turneth away wrath: but grievous words stir up anger" (Proverbs 15:1). In fact, ungodly words incite devilish actions; however, "The words of the Lord are pure words: as silver tried in a furnace of earth, purified seven times" (Psalm 12:6). There is a thin line between ungodly words and evil actions.

To be sure, everyone who says, "Lord, Lord," does not necessarily mean it. Since words matter, individuals should be very careful the words they utter to each other. This is precisely why the Bible declares "Let the words of my mouth, and the meditation of my heart (mind), be acceptable in thy sight, O Lord, my strength, and my redeemer" (Psalm 19:14). More importantly, every American should understand: "For as he thinketh in his heart, so is he: Eat and drink, saith he to thee; but his heart is not with thee" (Proverbs 23:7). Therefore, "Walk in wisdom toward them that are without, redeeming the time. Let your speech be always with grace, seasoned with salt, that ye may know how ye ought to answer every man" (Colossians 4:5-6). Hence, on both sides of the political equation when we operate out of written Scriptural words: we are on the Lord's side; we can all walk together; and we, most assuredly, give no place to the devil, for after all, "Can two walk together, except they be agreed?" (Amos 3: 3). America, be mindful and ever so careful, because we only have two choices: God and the devil. Hence, the real choices are spiritual choices, not the political choices of Democratic versus Republican.

And, just in case you have conveniently developed amnesia or mal-nutrition of the brain, please be reminded that the choice has already been established, stated, and emphatically declared with the precious blood already shed "That we hold these truths to be self-evident..." in America's Preamble to the Constitution and the Articles of the U.S. Constitution; after all, "There is no wisdom nor understanding nor counsel against the Lord" (Proverbs 23:7). The U.S. Constitution is a spiritual document written primarily by god-fearing men; therefore, the Constitution matters. Which do Americans love more: the Constitution or partisan politics?

As Americans, we all know that "Righteousness exalteth a nation: but sin is a reproach to any people" (Proverbs 14:34). And, through God's Word, we should all know that "The house of the wicked shall be overthrown: but the tabernacle of the upright shall flourish" (Proverbs 14:11). As men and women of God, let's embrace the will of God, and above all, the teachings of our Lord and Savior, Jesus Christ the Righteous One because ". . . we must all appear before the judgment seat of Christ; that every one may receive the things done in his body, according to that he hath done, whether it be good or bad" (2 Corinthians 5:10). Without a doubt, ". . . every one of us shall give an account of himself to God" (Romans 14:12). Therefore, through these Scriptural spiritual precepts, we should "Be not deceived: evil communications corrupt good manners. Awake to righteousness, and sin not; for some have not the knowledge of God: I speak this to your shame" (1 Corinthians 15:33-34).

We should always remember that no individual can hide from the Word of God; therefore, "Be not deceived; God is not mocked: for whatsoever a man soweth, that shall he also reap. For he that soweth to his flesh shall of the flesh reap corruption; but he that soweth to the Spirit shall of the Spirit reap life everlasting. And let us not be weary in well doing: for in due season we shall reap, if we faint not. As we have therefore opportunity; let us do good unto all men, especially unto them who are of the household of faith" (Galatians 6:7-10).

America's spiritual and political leadership problem is grounded in the inability of Christian pastoral leaders to foster a spiritual-focused moral ought. In Christendom, we have too many pastoral sell-outs: "His watchmen are blind: they are ignorant, they are all dumb dogs, they cannot bark; sleeping, lying down, loving to slumber" (Isaiah 56:10). Pastoral leaders are teaching and preaching what church goers want to hear, and not what they need to know spiritually. There is a spiritual heaven and hell. Make no mistake about it. Therefore, the worst place for your soul to ever reside eternally is in a spiritual hell especially after having lived in a physical hell on earth; hence, pastoral leaders embrace in totality the unadulterated Word of God, because "The word of God is quick, and powerful, and sharper than any two-edged sword" (Hebrews 4:12). It is written "Let us therefore come boldly unto the throne of grace, that we may obtain mercy, and find grace to help in time of need" (Hebrews 4:16).

For it is as certain as the sun rising in the east and setting in the west, ". . . it is appointed unto men once to die, but after this the judgment: so Christ was once offered to bear the sins of many; and unto them that look for him shall he appear the second time without sin unto salvation" (Hebrews 9:27-28). God is the judge, and "God judgeth the righteous, and God is angry with the wicked every day" (Psalm 7:11). Hear well, pastoral leaders: Foretold is forewarned. "The heads thereof judge for reward, and the priests thereof teach for hire, and the prophets thereof divine for money: yet will they lean upon the Lord, and say, Is not the Lord among us? none evil can come upon us" (Micah 3:11).

Christians, "Be sober, be vigilant; because your adversary the devil, as a roaring lion, walketh about, seeking whom he may devour: whom resist stedfast in the faith, knowing that the same afflictions are accomplished in your brethren that are in the world" (1 Peter 5:8-9). Pastoral leaders, God's desire is that you shepherd His people toward righteousness for Christ's sake; therefore, "Submit yourselves to God. Resist the devil, and he will flee from you" (James 4:7). Selah!

Why?

Telling the truth must always be the primary objective. It's not the story but the TRUTH. Without a doubt, the TRUTH belongs to God. And, it is written "All scripture is given by inspiration of God, and is profitable for doctrine, for reproof, for correction, for instruction in righteousness" (2 Timothy 3:16).

Any individual who reports on the truth should not create the circumstances or conditions for reporting the truth; hence, "The Lord gave the word: great was the company of those that published it" (Psalm 68:11). Moreover, "In the beginning was the Word, and the Word was with God, and the Word was God" (John 1:1). Any man can challenge another man, but no man should ever be foolish enough to challenge God who is the ultimate truth. Moreover, "There is no wisdom nor understanding against the Lord" (Proverbs 21:30). And, "There is a way that seemeth right unto a man, but the end thereof are the ways of death" (Proverbs 14:12).

This writer's spiritual thoughts are grounded in both theology as well as sociology. My graduate training (Syracuse University) was in the field of sociology, which in turn, became my profession (that is, means of earning a living for my family). But, my "labor-of-love" training in theology at Colgate Rochester Crozer Divinity School represents my heart, soul and love of the Word of God.

We know that "LIFE" has many twists and turns as well as ups and downs. Sociology is the study of society, that is, individuals learning to live in peace and harmony with each other in urbane-concrete-asphalt jungles. "Thou shalt love thy neighbor as thyself" (Mark 12:31). But our theology ought to be an expression of our spiritual desire for eternal life with God the TRUTH is God's Word: "Sanctify them through thy truth: thy word is truth" (John 17:17). There is no doubt about it, God is love. This is why we are commanded to "Love the Lord thy God with all thy heart, and with all thy soul, and with all thy mind, and with all thy strength" (Mark 12:30).

Now, what was once in the closet is openly being expressed in a bold-sinful-manner from Christian Right Evangelical church pulpits, to family dinner-room tables, to schoolhouse playgrounds, and even to The White House. Discussions in all of these instances have American society in spiritual conflict with God. God hates sin. Moreover, "God judgeth the righteous, and God is angry with the wicked every day" (Psalm 7:11).

America, know full well, "Thus saith the Lord; cursed be the man that trusteth in man, and maketh flesh his arm, and whose heart departed from the Lord" (Jeremiah 17:5). Therefore, beware of those among us who believe that it is alright for civilians to have military-style weaponry especially as spiritually confused as American society is presently. America is a democratic-multicultural society which, in turn, is governed primarily by white males who do not have the spiritual will or the moral courage to protect their own children from military-style weapons in our public schools and churches. Obviously, it is not minorities utilizing military-style weapons to commit mass murder. Think about it!

Black Americans, as well as other permanent tan minorities know full well that white men do not give a damn about your children. However, their children give a damn about themselves as well as other children. Just maybe, these young people will inspire their fathers and mothers toward a higher spiritual understanding that they are under siege. More importantly, their parents will begin to vote for politicians who have the spiritual-moral conscience to enact an assault weapons ban as well as vote against the vulgar monetary interests of the NRA. The children of Parkland, Florida, are publicly demonstrating to the world community that they have more spiritual commonsense than their parents, and most public officials who are proponents of American citizens possessing military-style weapons as though they are in a military unit.

The election of Donald J. Trump to the U.S. Presidency has brought to the forefront the most dreadful, shameful sin of American history, and that is, institutional racism as well as the issue of permanent tan minorities as second-class citizens. We now know that the Russians did interfere with the 2016 Presidential election, but the voters had everything to do with the election of an immoral man. Those Christian Right Evangelicals and Republican Party loyalists who voted for President Trump after he told the world about his spiritual-moral-character, and what he was going to do if elected, should now ask God for forgiveness. President Trump is many things, but the world knows that he is a chronic, habitual liar. "Six things doth the Lord hate; yea, seven are an abomination unto him: A proud look, a lying tongue, and hands that shed innocent blood" (Proverbs 6:16-17).

After the goodness of God to America (Home of the Brave and the Land of the Free), those who voted for President Trump ought to be ashamed of themselves for their complicity in the destruction of America's democratic institutions. After making such a horrific spiritual-moral-ungodly choice, in conjunction with President

Trump, just maybe you can spiritually redeem yourselves by protecting our children from military-style weapons, "For all have sinned, and come short of the glory of God" (Romans 3:23).

What does one individual killing another individual really accomplish, even in capital crimes? We all know ". . . it is appointed unto men once to die, but after this the judgment" (Hebrews 9:27). It is written, "Thou shalt not kill." And, without a doubt, "The house of the wicked shall be overthrown: but the tabernacle of the upright shall flourish" (Proverbs 14:11). The Republican Party in conjunction with Christian Right Evangelicals corrupted the spiritual-moral meaning of what America truly represents: The Free-Will Rights Of Others! Sin is sin. God hates all sins, and that is a fact! We should forever remember that the eternal Supreme Court is in Heaven with God, Jesus the Righteous One, and The Holy Spirit, not in Washington, D.C.

Because of the perpetration of extreme military-style gun violence in public schools and houses of worship, America's children are beginning to walk righteously and boldly in the spiritual light of God. "But if we walk in the light, as he is in the light, we have fellowship one with another, and the blood of Jesus Christ his Son cleanseth us from all sin" (1 John 1:7). President Trump, Christian Right Evangelicals, Republican Party Loyalists, and spiritually-confused minds about military-style guns in the hands of civilians, get on board; the train is coming. "Woe unto them! For they have gone in the way of Cain and ran greedily after the error of Balaam for reward, and perished in the gainsaying of Core" (Jude 1:11). Our children are not willing to be victimized by the spirit of Cain (that is, killing). For "Out of the mouth of babes and sucklings hast thou ordained strength because of thine enemies, that thou mightiest still the enemy and the avenger" (Psalm 8:2). Selah!

What's Next, America?

Are we going to twiddle our thumbs and give silent consent to the insanity of President Trump, while he literally destroys our democracy and democratic institutions? Of course, Christian Right Evangelicals and the Republican Party are co-conspirators in the White-Privilege-Racism game that is being played out in The White House! Let's say it again: Silence is consent. First of all, someone please inform President Trump that black individuals from "shit-hole" (S-Hole) countries in Africa assisted with the engineering design and provided the construction labor that built The White House. Moreover, the engineering design for the city streets of Washington, D.C. was performed by a black man (Benjamin Banneker) from the "S-Hole" Continent of Africa. Maybe this is why in President Trump's narrow-minded-way-of-thinking The White House is simply a "DUMP". Without a doubt, President Trump's intellectual capabilities, spiritual moral understanding, and acumen are proof-positive that the education gap is one of America's core social problems. It's no accident of history that the Founders created a mass universal educational system that all citizens might learn how to read the Bible. To be sure, President Trump is a successful, "con-artist" businessman, because he has truly conned Republican Party voters and Christian Right Evangelicals.

This question must be asked: Do Republican voters hate themselves, as well as, America so much that to feel good about being white; they will allow a "con-artist" to treat them like "A-Holes"? The Trumpster only called black and brown countries "S-Holes"; while, on the other hand, he treats Republican Party Officials/Voters and working class Whites, in general, like "A-Holes." At the same time, he orchestrates making the rich, richer, and poor whites, poorer. President Trump has taken the concept of "The Ugly American" to the nth degree. More importantly, Republicans and Christian Right Evangelicals, you have enabled the Trumpster in making America, NOT great, but a negative discussion point in the world community (The Ugly American)!

A good image is worth more than all the tea in China. Of course, God-fearing individuals know that "Fools make a mock at sin: but among the righteous there is favor" (Proverbs 14:9). Real Christians are not perplexed or troubled by President Trump's lack of spiritual-intellectual understanding, because they know that it is written in Heaven and eventually will be established on earth: "But many that are first shall be last; and the last shall be first" (Matthew 19:30). More importantly, real Americans know that our Constitutional founding is established upon Biblical principles, and born-again Christians know that it is difficult for a rich man to be spiritually redeemed, because: "It is easier for a camel to go through the eye of a needle, than for a rich man to enter into the kingdom of God" (Matthew 19:24). The Kingdom of God is about loving God and loving your neighbor as yourself, not loving money. "For the love of money is the root of all evil" (1 Timothy 6:10).

President Donald J. Trump is the News, and it is not good news, but it is the News even though sad as it is. Apparently, President Trump has conveniently forgotten that his parents emigrated from a foreign country where they lacked developmental opportunities to "The Land of the Free and the Home of the brave" in search of a better quality of life. His father acquired that better-quality-of-life for his family through real estate development, and he became economically successful. He then sent his son (Donald) to one of the best business colleges to obtain a business degree. Thus, according to President Trump, his father loaned, but we all know, his father gave him one million dollars to go into the real estate business. Moreover, we know that Trump does not pay his debts (four bankruptcies). When his father died, he left an estate of at least two hundred million dollars, which in turn, is called a "silver-spoon in the mouth".

But, unfortunately, in his narrow-minded way of thinking, President Trump views himself as a successful businessman, even though he has filed bankruptcy four times. He lost his own money as well as portions of his family's fortune. In a panic mode, he began borrowing money from anyone and everywhere, including from Russia and China. It is one thing to file financial bankruptcy, but it is another to have the entire world come to understand that you are spiritually and morally bankrupt as well as corrupt. Unfortunately, the silence of Republican Party Officials and Christian Right Evangelicals makes them co-conspirators in Presidential-Moral-Bankruptcy and built upon a foundation of institutional lying, and personal wrong doing. How do you know when President Trump is lying? Answer: because his lips are moving.

America is a nation that institutionalized a system of "White Privilege" off of the backs of slave laborers from the "S-Hole" Continent of Africa. Lest we forget, America's physical infra-structure was built off of the backs of free African-American-Labor: The White use of Blacks. Now, some white Americans no longer feel the need for or desire to have Blacks remain in America: "Make America White Again." Scientifically and technologically, American society has advanced beyond the need for physical/manual labor simply, because machines and robots can perform needed common labor tasks. The Trump Presidency represents the collapse of ethical-moral-norms of civility and human decency. In fact, The Trump circus in The White House has replaced Ringling Brothers and Barnum and Bailey Circus (Greatest Show on Earth) as entertainment in American culture. The only problem is, this replacement comes with horrendous national and international consequences and catapults the Trump Circus to the "Greatest Screw-Up on Earth."

Christian Right Evangelicals especially those of you who are doctrinally of a sound spiritual mind, please take the time to explain to President Trump who Christians truly are: "What know ye not that your body is the temple of the Holy Ghost which is in you, which ye have of God, and ye are not your own? For ye are bought with a price: therefore glorify God in your body, and in your spirit, which are God's" (1 Corinthians 6:19 20). Recently, President Trump had his annual physical exam by governmental medical professionals, and they concluded and reported to the American people that President Trump is of "sound mind" and "healthy body." However, he has, without a doubt, demonstrated to the entire world, that he is spiritually sick, because he is a liar and the truth is not in him. "Frowardness (contrariness) is in his heart, he deviseth mischief continually; he soweth discord. Therefore shall his calamity come suddenly; suddenly shall he be broken without remedy. These six things doth the Lord hate: yea, seven are an abomination unto him: a proud look, a lying tongue, and hands that shed innocent blood, an heart that deviseth wicked imaginations, feet that be swift in running to mischief, A false witness that speaketh lies, and he that soweth discord among the brethren" (Proverbs 6:14-19). Selah! What Happened to Quality And Pride in American Society?

Have our individualistic-ultra egos destroyed our spiritual-moral conscience concerning what is right and what is wrong? Seemingly, too many Americans are attempting to make right, wrong and wrong, right, and make it work. America, let's get off of this spiritual road to oblivion, the Trump Band-Wagon, which is taking us into the wilderness of spiritual ignorance where there is no return. "Be not deceived; God is not mocked; for whatsoever a man soweth, that shall he also reap. For he that soweth to his flesh shall of his flesh reap corruption; but he that soweth to the Spirit shall of the Spirit reap life everlasting" (Galatians 6:7). Hence, Christian Right Evangelicals, "Be sober, be vigilant; because your adversary the devil, as a roaring lion, walketh about, seeking whom he may devour: whom resist stedfast in the faith, knowing that the same afflictions are accomplished in your brethren that are in the world" (1 Peter 5:8-9). Of course, this is precisely why every Christian Right Evangelical should prick his/her own spiritual conscience and

"Submit yourselves therefore to God. Resist the devil, and he will flee from you" (James 4:7).

The greatest social democracy on the planet should not be characterized by spiritual-moral confusion, because confusion is of the devil, not of God. Moreover, Christian Right Evangelicals, the Bible is prophecy; therefore, "This know also, that in the last days perilous times shall come. For men shall become lovers of their own selves, covetous, boasters, proud, blasphemers, disobedient to parents, unthankful, unholy, without natural affection, trucebreakers, false accusers, incontinent, fierce, despisers of those that are good, traitors, heady, high minded, lovers of pleasures more than lovers of God; having a form of godliness, but denying the power thereof: from such turn away" (2 Timothy 3:1-5). America, we know that this Scripture is applicable to most Republicans, because they are completely spiritually confused in their thinking about what is going on in American society. Just maybe their confusion is a result of their own elitist attitudes, and above all, their blind loyalty to the leadership style of President Trump.

Christian Right Evangelicals and secular-minded individuals of the same socio-economic-political mentality, and who unfortunately believe in privilege-based-democracy, not equal is equal democracy. Therefore, please know that EGO is a personal-pronoun-disease acronym for "Edge-God-Out." But, on the other hand, faithful Christians who have a personal relationship with God through His Son, Jesus Christ the Righteous One, know that they should "Let the words of my mouth, and the meditation of my heart, be acceptable in thy sight, O Lord, my strength, and my redeemer" (Psalm 19:14).

America and especially Christian Right Evangelicals, take heed, and please remind President Trump of the Good News Gospel recorded in these Scriptural verses. "Submit yourselves therefore to God. Resist the devil, and he will flee from you." (James 4:7). Because: "A little that a righteous man hath is better than the riches of many wicked." (Psalm 37: 16). Therefore, "Leaving the principles of the doctrine of Christ, let us go on unto perfection; not laying again the foundation of repentance from dead works, and of faith toward God, and of the doctrine of baptisms, and of laying on of hands, and the resurrection of the dead, and of eternal judgment. And this will we do, if God permit." (Hebrews 6:1-3). Yes, President Trump, money and power are important material instruments, but they are not the cornerstones principles of a great society. Spirituality and morality are eternal spiritual dimensions for greatness for any nation-state. Great societies usually collapse from within, because of spiritual-moral decay, not because of external forces. Morality cannot be legislated or enforced with weaponry (guns). On 9/11, America was physically attacked by foreign adversaries. But, on 11/9 the eighty-one percent (81%) of Christian Right Evangelicals who voted for Donald J. Trump spiritually attacked American social democracy. The Roman Empire collapsed primarily because of spiritual-moral-bankrupt leadership, not because of a lack of power and money.

Prior to November 8th, 2016, all of America's Presidential leaders knew how to speak spiritual truth to power, not threaten war or nuclear annihilation. Christian Right Evangelicals, please spiritually understand what truth-sanctification is all about. "Sanctify them through thy truth; thy word is truth" (John 17:17). In so doing, you just might be able to spiritualize/civilize the tongue of President Trump since the issues of "Death and life are in the power of the tongue" (Proverbs 18:12). Spirituality and morality must be taught and exampled in family structures (homes), churches, and schools. The spiritual-moral breakdown that is plaguing American society is primarily because of the breakdown of family structure, the spiritual-moral failure of Christian Right Evangelical leadership and their greed for power, money, and material empire building, the spiritual breakdown of the teaching of the 3-Rs in public education (Christian-Moral Society), the systematic curriculum-disrespect of non-white cultures, and the White-Privilege-oriented polarization of the criminal justice system. Lady Justice has been found not to be blind! Nor are the scales of justice equally applied and enforced.

Again, the spiritual-moral breakdown of America's primary institutions is at the crux of our internal confusion as well as our moral-leadership-decline vacuum in the world community:

1. The inability of American families to teach/example godly love and train children in the way of the Lord. "And if it seem evil unto you to serve the Lord, choose you this day whom ye will serve; whether the gods which your fathers served that were on the other side of the flood, or the gods of the Amorites, in whose land ye dwell: but as for me and my house, we will serve the Lord" (Joshua 24:15).

2. The inability of Christian Right Evangelical pastors to preach and teach the Gospel of the Good News according to the spiritual principles of Jesus Christ the Righteous One. Pastoral leaders are spiritually charged with leading individuals into God's truth, because it is in God that individuals find salvation. "For if a man know not how to rule his own house, how shall he take care of the church of God?" (1 Timothy 3:5).

3. The inability of public and private school educators to teach and example excellence in achievement in conjunction with ethical-moral values. All education is moral education. "Blessed is he that readeth, and they that hear the words of this prophecy, and keep those things which are written therein: for the time is at hand" (Revelation 1:3).

4. America's political governance problem(s) concerning socio-economic ills cannot be solved through the barrel of guns—only

through diplomatic channels. "Put up again thy sword into his place: for all they that take the sword shall perish with the sword" (Matthew 26:52).

5. Lady Justice is not blind, nor are her scales balanced, and oftentimes she peaks at skin-color and bank accounts. The greatest law(s) comes from Heaven, not earth. Unfortunately, the civil and criminal laws of American society are based upon White Privilege, but "The law of the Spirit of life in Christ Jesus hath made me free from the law of sin and death. For what the law could not do, in that it was weak through the flesh, God sending his own Son in the likeness of sinful flesh, and for sin, condemned sin in the flesh" (Romans 8:2-3). America, there is no excuse for sin (unrighteousness). Selah!

Lies, Lies, and More Lies!

The Bible emphatically declares that no God-fearing individual should lie especially "Thou shalt not bear false witness against thy neighbor" (Exodus 20:16). It has rightly been said there are three types of lies: lies, damn lies, and how to lie utilizing statistics. Of course, there are lies and more lies that come from the mouth of ungodly individuals. The Bible declares that the beginning of all sin is a lie. "For God is not the author of confusion (LIES), but of peace, as in all churches of the saints" (1 Corinthians 14:33). More importantly, "Ye are of your father the devil, and the lusts of your father ye will do. He was a murderer from the beginning, and abode not in the truth, because there is no truth in him. When he speaketh a lie, he speaketh of his own: for he is a liar, and the father of it" (John 8:44). Question: how do you know when President Trump is lying? Answer: when his lips are moving!

President Trump is a professional-chronic-habitual-liar to the nth degree at employing all three types of lies in his quest for absolute-dictatorial-power. Republicans have desired the Presidential power to govern for eight years, and now they have not only the Office of the Presidency, but the majority in both the House of Representatives and the Senate Chamber. Now that they have all three branches of governmental authority under their leadership; they know what they want to do: make the rich, richer and the poor, poorer. But, they can't do it because they are too busy covering up President Trump's lies. Above all, Republicans do not know how to govern with democratic fairness. Their desire is to simply govern with conservatism (exclusion) without spiritual-moral-intellectual-conscience-integrity. Republicanism without spiritual-moral-conscience was a recipe for electing a professional liar to the Office of the President. Now that they have it, what in the hell are they going to do with it; especially with a professional liar as the President? Without a doubt, President Trump has surrounded himself with a professional political director and a team of go-along-to-get-along lie accommodators. To be sure, if it were not for a "Free-Press" with intellectual integrity, America would have to wonder where she would be with Donald J. Trump as President.

Their talk is cheap. This is why President Trump declared we didn't know that healthcare was so complicated. Of course, social-democracy-political governance is much more difficult to achieve in a society, because it requires equality of opportunity for all and not just White Nationalistic Privilege. More than practically anything else, democracy requires political leaders who are willing to tell the truth, the whole truth, and nothing but the truth so help them God, not foster a Sanhedrin Council of automatons who are willing to become lie accommodators. In case you are not familiar with the work of the Sanhedrin Council: Remember the Condemnation of Jesus.

The poor will always be with us because, invariably, the rich become greedy, and above all, the poor help to make the rich, rich. Unfortunately, the rich want more, they need more, and above all, they have-to-have more. "And he said unto them, Take heed, and beware of covetousness: for a man's life consisteth not in the abundance of the things which he possesseth. And he spake a parable unto them, saying, The ground of a certain rich man brought forth plentifully: And he thought within himself, saying, What shall I do, because I have no room where to bestow my fruits? And he said, This will I do: I will pull down my barns, and build greater; and there will I bestow all my fruits and goods. And I will say to my soul, Soul, thou hast much goods laid up for many years; take thine ease, eat, drink, and be merry. But God said unto him, Thou fool, this night thy soul shall be required of thee: then whose shall those things be, which thou hast provided? So is he that layeth up treasure for himself, and is not rich toward God" (Luke 12:15-21).

It is more profitable for an individual to have a rich relationship with God than to possess tons of silver and gold. In President Trump's mind, he wants America to be in the same trick-bag he is in with Putin and Russia; where they ultimately would become co-dictators of the world-community. This is precisely why the Secretary of State is silent and has dismissed top career professional diplomats who have been employed in the State department for more than twenty years.

Seemingly, these are the first stages of a world-governing-conspiracy operating between President Trump and Putin. They desire to control the human and physical resources of the world community. Putin desires to control the Eastern countries with Germany as the "plum" caveat. President Trump will then control the West and the rest of the world community. However, President Trump will soon discover that the East and Germany are not enough, because Putin wants to control the whole world. Putin knows that there can only be one dictator (El Supremo). "For as he thinketh in his heart, so is he: Eat and drink, saith he to thee; but his heart is not with thee" (Proverbs 23:7). Let the good times roll. For after all, President Trump will find this truism out the hard way because a hard head makes a soft behind. Neither President Trump nor Dictator Putin has compassion for their fellow countrymen; they only want to use their fellow countrymen as pawns in a chess game for power and material riches. Behold, America, you have been told; therefore, "Let it be written; Let it be done." Stop the madness now; unless you are insane.

God has a sovereign will, and He has a permissive will. President Donald J. Trump is a spiritual reflection of God's permissive will. God allowed Donald J. Trump to be elected President. God is seeking to get America's undivided attention, for America is destroying herself from within, because of her evil thinking about racial and ethnic superiority, her lust for power, and her insatiable love and greed for money by both political and religious leaders. "Nevertheless the foundation of God standeth sure, having this seal, The Lord knoweth them that are his. And, Let everyone that nameth the name of Christ depart from iniquity" (2 Timothy 2:19). America, get right! Live right for the time is at hand. Prepare for the judgment of God. "So then every one of us shall give account of himself to God" (Romans 14:12). Beware, therefore, of promises made by liars. God gave Noah the rainbow sign, no more water, but fire next time. Selah!

Lying Does Not Alter Reality

There is no such thing as alternative reality based upon alternative facts. The Bible teaches us clearly what alternative facts are: "But shun profane and vain babblings: for they will increase unto more ungodliness" (2 Timothy 2:16). There is only truth based upon God's reality, not individual and institutional lying because equal is equal, not more or less equal. In our Christian churches, we know this spiritual truth, but we cannot live the reality of this eternal truth. "Woe unto you, scribes and Pharisees, Hypocrites! For ye pay tithe of mint and anise and cumin, and have omitted the weightier matters of the law, judgment, mercy, and faith: these ought ye to have done, and not leave the other undone. Ye blind guides, which strain at a gnat, and swallow a camel" (Matthew 23:23-24). Foretold is forewarned, Christian Right Evangelicals.

Moreover, ultimate reality is reality as God intended it to be because

"The earth is the Lord's, and the fullness thereof; the world, and they that dwell therein" (Psalm 24:1). The irreverent lying of Trump Administration Officials is leading America into a state of utter moral chaos and spiritual confusion and will ultimately end in war. If individuals continue to play with fire, eventually you will be burned, and your children will be burned as well. "These six things doth the Lord hate: yea, seven are an abomination unto him: A proud look, a lying tongue, and hands that shed innocent blood" (Proverbs 6:16-17). The question of all questions is: Can anything good come out of Trump Tower via The White House? It does not appear to be so given what we have seen and heard since January 20th, 2017, because lies operate off of borrowed energy, and the truth creates its own energy on which it stands alone.

The White House has been transformed into "The House of Lies." Systemic serial lying by Trump Officials has produced the Rule of Trump, not the Rule of Law based upon democratic tenets. Democracy is built upon the Rule of Law, and above all, truth telling. President Trump's amoral approach to governance is based upon a businessman's agenda which includes the few and excludes the many. Democracy is of the people, by the people, and for the people. The Trump Administration agenda is not a citizen agenda. This is why President Trump views trade as a zero-sum game rather than a mutual-benefit game. Moreover, Trump officials do not understand that if individuals tell the truth; they do not have to try to remember (recall) what they said. Here's the long and short of it: "For the law of the Spirit of life in Christ Jesus hath made me free from the law of sin and death" (Romans 8:2).

Trump Administration Officials, stop lying! We all should know and know without a doubt that "Righteousness exalteth a nation: but sin is a reproach to any people" (Proverbs 14:34). Lying is the beginning of sin, and individuals should not bear false witness against one another. Shame! Shame! Shame on you, President Trump for lying for General Flynn, and lying on former FBI Director Comey. Christian Right Evangelicals, since you voted for President Trump, please inform him that "There is no wisdom nor understanding nor counsel against the Lord" (Proverbs 21:30). America, pray for the Trump Administration, for "If my people, which are called by my name, shall humble themselves, and pray, and seek my face, and turn from their wicked ways; then will I hear from heaven, and will forgive their sin, and will heal their land" (2 Chronicles 7:14).

Seemingly, the approach to democratic governance by Trump Officials is based upon lower-class-value constructs (Gutter Rats) rather than middle-class-democratic values. America has entered into an era of government-by-personality rather than democratic institutional policies and procedures which, in turn, are grounded in time-honored, democratic tenets. The integrity of America's democratic institutions and political system of governance is slowly drifting into ungodly partisan politics. By the way, this is why so many Americans commonly believe that politics is a pile-of-manure, and, consequently, do not participate in the political (electoral) process (vote).

Alternative facts ultimately entice individuals into sinning against God, self, and country. Above all, this is precisely why individuals must always remember that "A wise man feareth, and departed from evil: but the fool rageth, and is confident" (Proverbs 14:16). Jesus is physically gone, but it's not goodbye, because some of us shall be caught up in the blinking of an eye in the sky with our Lord and Savior Jesus Christ. Therefore, all Americans must clearly understand that alternative facts are grounded in lying, and therefore, we must spiritually guard ourselves against carnal mindedness and resist the unreality of alternative facts "For to be carnally minded is death; but to be spiritually minded is life and peace. Because the carnal mind is enmity against God: for it is not subject to the law of God, neither indeed can be. So then they that are in the flesh cannot please God" (Romans 8:6-8).

The rule of law is the spiritual cornerstone principle of social democracy. It is obedience to law which invariably preserves the integrity of democratic governmental institutions: Government of laws versus Government of men. Moreover, my fellow Americans, God is not mocked nor is He fooled; individuals reap what they sow. Therefore, understand "Nevertheless the foundation of God standeth sure, having this seal, The Lord knoweth them that are his. And, Let everyone that nameth the name of Christ depart from iniquity (sin)" (2 Timothy 2:19).

Republicans, this is not a sermonette, but a spiritual reminder of the power of the Word of God; therefore, understand and embrace this spiritual truism: "There is a way which seemeth right unto a man, but the end thereof are the ways of death" (Proverbs 14:12). The Republican Party is being victimized by ungodly group thinking and hi-jacked by White-Privilege-Oriented Nationalism. The spirit of Abraham Lincoln is probably aggrieved at the pathetic desire of most Republicans for power, privilege, and money without collective responsibility for the well-being of the greatest democratic nation on the planet. Just a spiritual reminder: "The house of the wicked shall be overthrown: but the tabernacle of the upright shall flourish" (Proverbs 14:11). The world is watching in utter dismay at what is being said and done by the Trump Administration, but more importantly, God has pure eyes; He sees and hears everything at the same time. "Thou art of purer eyes than to behold evil, and canst not look on iniquity, wherefore lookest thou upon them that deal treacherously, and holdest thy tongue when the wicked devoureth the man that is more righteous than he?" (Habakkuk 1:13). The bad joke in The White House has become America's horrible nightmare on 1600 Pennsylvania Avenue. Selah!

Is Life All About Money?

If it is, God help us! No one is seeking to be judgmental, not even the Great Book of Life. It is an individual's own moral conscience that does the judging, because ultimately "God judgeth the righteous, and God is angry with the wicked every day" (Psalm 7:11). The objective is simply to bring to the moral conscience of God-fearing Americans that ". . . the love of money is the root of all evil: which while some coveted after, they have erred from the faith, and pierced themselves through with many sorrows" (I Timothy 6:10). Because "He who loves money will not be satisfied with money, nor he who loves abundance with its income" (Ecclesiastes 5:10 NASB). President Trump in an ungodly manner has chosen to inject devilish confusion into the national debate concerning Civil Rights (The First Amendment) and police brutality against minorities especially Black Americans. Kneeling is an honorable position which gives God the honor and the glory in all things. Seemingly, this positional form of godly prostration is one that President Trump is not familiar with. Every day men and women in the U.S. Military system risk their lives in defense of the Human Rights and Civil Rights of all Americans. If this is not the case, we need to change the U.S. Constitution. Therefore, as a society, America should not arbitrarily strip individuals of their human rights because of a disagreement with the lawful protest Constitutional processes employed.

Adding to the spiritual-moral confusion, the owner of the Dallas Cowboys, Jerry Jones, has injected the issue of financial gain (money) into the spiritual-moral equation of First Amendment Rights. Mr. Jones' rationale for his money-making position is simply this: "It is all about the bottom-line economics (money)." We all know why President Trump jumped in the fray of a First Amendment Rights issue to change the narrative from Civil Rights to disrespecting whites. Of course, most Christian Right Evangelicals went for the okey-dokie because of the racial makeup of the NFL. Most assuredly, a round object cannot be placed in a square hole, but we all should "Take heed, and beware of covetousness: for a man's life consisteth not in the abundance of the things which he possesseth" (Luke 12:15).

Without a doubt, President Trump is a vulgar businessman who does not know how to love and serve God by loving and serving others. Four (4) bankruptcies are not spiritual-moral characteristics of a good, moral businessman. By the way, always lying and scandalizing others are not qualities of a God-fearing individual simply, because God hates a lying tongue: "A proud look, a lying tongue, and hands that shed innocent blood." (Proverbs 6:17).

Every individual must sacrifices, because life is about sacrifices. But how do we ensure that every individual is indeed sacrificing? Unfortunately, Jerry Jones is demanding that pro-football- players sacrifice their Constitutional Civil Rights to peacefully protest social injustices so both can make money. Of course, Mr. Jones makes more money than the entire football operation, because he has a sweetheart-low-tax-paying deal. If football players are willing to give up their First Amendment Rights, is Mr. Jones willing to reduce the price of ticket sales, football paraphernalia, parking fees, food, beverages, and pay more in taxes? I don't think so.

Christian Right Evangelicals, the Scripture below is why the owner of the Dallas Cowboys is not willing to make the sacrifices listed above. Behold Jesus' words to the rich young man who came to Him and said, "Good Master, what good thing shall I do that I may have eternal life? Jesus answered by saying: Why callest me good? There is none good but one, that is, God: but if thou wilt enter into life, keep the commandments. . . . The young man saith unto him, All these things have I kept from my youth up: what lack I yet? Jesus said unto him, go sell that thou hast, and give to the poor, and thou shalt have treasure in heaven: and come and follow me. But when the young man heard that saying, he went away sorrowful: for he had great possessions. Then Jesus said unto his disciples, Verily I say unto you, That a rich man shall hardly enter into the Kingdom of heaven. And again I say unto you, it is easier for a camel to go through the eye of a needle, than for a rich man to enter into the Kingdom of God" (Matthew 19:16-23).

Christian Right Evangelicals, this is why if any individual lacks wisdom, let him ask God, because God is speaking to us through His servant James says, "If any of you lack wisdom, let him ask of God that giveth to all men liberally, and upbraideth not; and it shall be given him. But let him ask in faith, nothing wavering, For he that wavereth is like a wave of the sea driven with the wind and tossed. For let not that man think that he shall receive any thing of the Lord. A double minded man is unstable in all of his ways" (James 1:5-8).

Initially, Mr. Jones knelt with the players highlighting their First Amendment Rights (cause) to make money. Now, he is emphatically insisting that Dallas Cowboy players stand, so that they can make money with him rather than kneel in dignity for themselves. In other words, stand or get fired. Hence, it is all about the principle of making money, not the spiritual (human) rights of others. Similarly, the most unprepared President in the history of American society is utilizing the Office of President to make money. President Trump's desire is not to faithfully serve a great nation because of its founding documents (Preamble and U.S. Constitution), but to reestablish a White-Privilege-Oriented America: Make America Great "White" Again.

Take heed, President Trump's America and those who want something for nothing: "Righteousness exalts a nation: but sin is a reproach to any people" (Proverbs 14:34). All of this spiritual-moral-political confusion is being orchestrated in conjunction with hypocritical Christian Right Evangelicals and their superficial misguided interpretation of Christianity: "Professing themselves to be wise, they became fools" (Romans 1:22). More importantly, "For God is not the author of confusion, but of peace, as in all churches of the saints" (1 Corinthians 14:33). America, even Jesus Christ the Righteous One had difficulty explaining to self-righteous individuals "Blessed are the peacemakers, for they shall be called sons of God" (Matthew 5:9).

Christian Right Evangelicals, are you part of the churches of the saints? Or are you part of churches of darkness? Of course, spiritual confusion has been flourishing in America for almost 400 years. Slavery was and is spiritual confusion. Most Americans believe that life is about God, family, and country (service to others); hence, the spiritual concept of "I am my brother's keeper" is America's credo simply because "We hold these truths to be self-evident, that all Men are created equal, that they are endowed by their Creator with certain unalienable Rights, that among these are Life, Liberty, and the Pursuit of Happiness." Unfortunately, there are some fellow Americans who refuse, or they cannot spiritually live in accordance with these moral principles and precepts. They ask the Cain question: "Am I my brother's keeper?" Their response is invariably: "Who is my brother?" Are we Cain's children? Or are we children of God? Selah!

Who Are You Listening To?

Listening is a Godly quality. This is why God demands that we listen as well as act in righteousness towards each other. Of course, if we properly listen to each other, we will better understand one another. Jesus said, "Blessed are they that hear the word of God, and keep it" (Luke 11:28). There is only one important small-still, quiet inner voice that all individuals must always listen to, because it is what brings individuals into the truth and reality of God. It is that small, still, inner, quiet voice that we must listen to says, "So then faith cometh by hearing, and hearing by the word of God" (Romans 10:17). As Christians, we must "Study to shew thyself approved unto God, a workman that needeth not to be ashamed, rightly dividing the word of truth" (2 Timothy 2:15). Moreover, individuals must be able to discern the truth from a lie by always listening to the still, inner, quiet voice of God.

Republican Party Officials and President Trump, beware of saying, "Lord, Lord," while running with the devil. Saying "Lord, Lord" with words but not with deeds is a dangerous, hellish, immoral proposition. This is why Jesus said to the disciples, "Take heed what ye hear: with what measure ye mete, it shall be measured to you: and unto you that hear shall more be given" (Mark 4:24). The spiritual reference point for Jesus' remarks to the disciples is the Two Great Commandments especially the Second Commandment: "Thou shalt love thy neighbor as thyself" (Matthew 22:39).

President Trump and his co-conspirators, are undermining America's democratic institutions; therefore: "Be not deceived; God is not mocked: for whatsoever a man soweth, that shall he also reap" (Galatians 6:7). Christian Right Evangelicals, you should heed this Scripture: "Lay hands suddenly on no man, neither be a partaker of other men's sins, keep thyself pure" (1 Timothy 5:22). Therefore, Christian Right Evangelicals, you embraced Trumpism too quickly, and as a Christian (Christ-like) you should have known better, because you should be listening to that small, still, inner, quiet voice (God). So, stop making ungodly excuses for this extremely ungodly male, because a Christian knows that: "A double minded man is unstable in all his ways" (James 1:8). Furthermore, this is why the Bible states emphatically "Let this mind be in you, which was also in Christ Jesus" (Philippians 2:5).

The breakdown of family life structure in American society has produced a monumental, spiritual, listening developmental problem, because what is taught, heard, and exampled in homes is displayed in America's socio-economic-culture. Parental spiritual guidance and the moral development of children are extremely important value orientations for the survival and well-being of any society; since society begins and ends in family. Without a doubt, too many of America's children are growing up listening to the drumbeat of secular, humanistic culture that is oriented towards (Me, Myself, and I) or instant gratification. Real Christians know that the sins of the fathers will produce a crooked and perverse nation. For example: children killing children. Sin is lawlessness. "Whosoever committeth sin transgresseth also the law: for sin is the transgression of the law" (1 John 3:4).

Technology is a modernistic blessing, and at the same time, a devilish curse, because too many Americans are growing up spiritually and morally undisciplined. Our children know more about computers, emailing, smart-phones, Face-Book, and texting while driving than they know about the principles, precepts, and concepts in the books from Genesis to Revelation. Couple this spiritual fact of family-life dysfunction with America's gun culture, and what you have is a society on the brink of self-annihilation.

Therefore, it should be of no surprise to anyone that as a society, we have gun violence in schools and churches. Guns very seldom protect individuals from injury or death. Unfortunately, guns are weapons of choice that are always used to inflict harm and death.

Certainly, in every family, there should be a prayer-in-time because the family that prays together stays together. Prayer is extremely important, because it is internal self-introspection. Prayer helps individuals learn how to live from the inside to the outside rather than vice-versa. Above all, there should be Bible study time to reinforce Biblical precepts and family-spiritual values. Every American family should understand this Scriptural admonition: "Be sober, be vigilant, because your adversary the devil, as a roaring lion, walketh about, seeking whom he may devour: whom resist steadfast in the faith, knowing that the same afflictions are accomplished in your brethren that are in the world" (1 Peter 5:8-9). This is precisely why King Solomon said, "Hearken unto thy father that begat thee, and despise not thy mother when she is old" (Proverbs 23:22). Children cannot and will not hearken (listen) to absentee, irresponsible fathers who are not willing to meet their basic survival needs (food, clothing, and shelter). Neither will children respect vanity-oriented mothers.

The mind is a state of being, and this is precisely why the Bible declares that the "Mind that was in Christ Jesus ought to also be in every human being." Here's why. In analyzing the concept "human being," we understand that the concept human is a compound word. Hue means dirt. Individuals have bodies made from dirt and the body shall return to the dirt: Ashes to ashes and dust to dust (Genesis 2:7; 3:19; Job 34:15, and Psalm 103:14). Man denotes mind. God gives each individual his/her own mind (free-will individuality); mind is a state of being (invisible-thinking-thoughts). "Being" is a spiritual concept that is grounded in the concept of ontology (God-Spirituality). Therefore, "Being" (divinity) is eternal, and thus, never dies.

Christian Right Evangelicals and Republican Party Loyalists, it's never too late to cease practicing self-righteous-hypocrisy: "Professing themselves to be wise, they became fools, and changed the glory of God into an image made like to corruptible man" (Romans 1:22). Practicing and seeking to perpetuate White Privilege under the guise of "draining the swamp" and perpetuating conservative values is an abomination to God. A word to the wise is sufficient. Hence, for Christ's (righteousness) sake leave President Trump alone, and "Submit yourselves therefore to God. Resist the devil, and he will flee from you" (James 4:7). More importantly, stop being so greedy because "A little that a righteous man hath is better than the riches of many wicked" (Psalm 37:16). Finally, Christian

Right Evangelicals and Christian Americans, pray that you "Grow in grace, and knowledge of our Lord and Savior Jesus Christ. To him be glory both now and forever. Amen" (2 Peter 3:18). Selah!

Intellectual Talent: Moral Character

Let's understand and spiritually be perfectly clear about covetousness as sin. For after all, covetousness can easily breakdown an individual's spiritual-moral-character or God-consciousness. Covetousness will entice individuals to do foolish, stupid, and ungodly things. Ask the three UCLA basketball players. It has rightly been said that an individual's intellectual talent should not take him or her to a place-status position in life whereby moral character cannot keep him/her. "But he that knew not, and did not commit things worthy of stripes, shall be beaten with few stripes. For unto whomsoever much is given, of him shall be much required: and to whom men have committed much, of him they will ask the more" (Luke 12:48).

In this Scriptural verse, Jesus tells us how individuals ought to live spiritually until; He returns. Hence, every Christian should be on the spiritual look-out for Jesus especially pastoral leaders, because they are the spiritual watchmen over our souls. Christian Right Evangelical pastoral leaders as well as all other pastoral leaders must give an account to God. Moreover, every Christian is required to work diligently for the Kingdom of God on earth as well as faithfully obey God's commandments, "For the law of the Spirit of life in Christ Jesus hath made me free from the law of sin and death. For what the law could not do, in that it was weak through the flesh, God sending his own Son in the likeness of sinful flesh, and for sin, condemned sin in the flesh: that the righteousness of the law might be fulfilled in us, who walk not after the flesh, but after the Spirit" (Romans 8:2-4).

American society has spiritually and morally come unglued primarily because of the breakdown of the nuclear family unit. Family units begin and end with Spiritual God-consciousness, not economic materialism (things). Moreover, society begins and ends in family units as designed by God, not family structure as decreed by the U.S. Supreme Court. America, "Take heed, and beware of covetousness: for a man's life consisteth not in the abundance of the things which he possesseth" (Luke 12:15). Life is about God, family, friends, church, and country. Power corrupts, and absolute power corrupts absolutely.

Hence, when life becomes a search for maximizing the pleasure principle; life ultimately becomes a ball of moral confusion as reflected in the sociology of Soap-Box-Operas: The Young and the Restless, The Bold and the Beautiful, the General Hospital looking for an emergency, and Days of Our Lives. And, in the distant past (1964-1999): On the Edge of Night, Searching for Tomorrow, As the World Turns, Another World, Guiding Light, One Life to Live, All of My Children, and The Secret Storm. The Secret Storm has created a spiritual-moral storm of monumental proportions. Soap Operas represent spiritual-moral confusion in first-class physical environments. The ungodly public exposure of PMS (the love of power, money and sex) among rich economically-politically-powerful men is the end results of the cultural "materializing-thingifying" of American life as vulgarly expressed in the desire to maximize sexual pleasure.

Without a doubt, America has become a pleasure-seeking culture. Individuals with power and money feel they have the power-privilege of receiving pleasure from anyone, anytime, with or without permission. Women are not the "sexual-pleasure-property" of men. Women are children of God. Herein lies the problem of powerful, ungodly men sexually harassing women, other men, and even children. This social-behavioral pattern is without spiritual-moral-conscience, and it must cease now, because we need a more spiritual-moral American culture. By the way, powerful men feel that the law does not apply to them, because they are the creators and enforcers of the law.

The Bible emphatically makes it crystal clear: "Whosoever committeth sin transgresseth also the law: for sin is the transgression of the law" (1 John 3:4). All unrighteousness is sin. Fellow Americans, we all must "Be sober, be vigilant; because your adversary the devil, as a roaring lion, walketh about, seeking whom he may devour: whom resist stedfast in the faith, knowing that the same afflictions are accomplished in your brethren that are in the world" (1 Peter 5:8-9), and that includes nuclear family members, Christian Right Evangelicals, politicians, and Hollywood. Know full well, America: "Be not deceived: evil communication corrupt good manners" (1 Corinthians 15:33). After all, ". . . she that liveth in pleasure is dead while she liveth" (1 Timothy 5:6). America, let's fully understand that no individual can get something for nothing, unless the desire is for nothing, and nothing from nothing leaves nothing. Therefore, "Be not deceived; God is not mocked: for whatsoever a man soweth, that shall he also reap. For he that soweth to his flesh shall of his flesh reap corruption; but he that soweth to the Spirit shall of the Spirit reap life everlasting" (Galatians 6:7-8).

The voices of all Americans should never be silenced by the wealth of billionaires, because "A little that a righteous man hath is better than the riches of many wicked" (Psalm 37:16). Jesus makes it very clear: "For what shall it profit a man, if he shall gain the whole world, and lose his own soul? Or what shall a man give in exchange for his soul? (Mark 8:36-37). All Americans should know this: "For as he thinketh in his heart, so is he" (Proverbs 23:7). Individuals must first think evil before translating evil thoughts into evil deeds. Jesus has assured all of us, spiritually, "For the wages of sin is death; but the gift of God is eternal life through Jesus Christ our Lord" (Romans 6:23).

As we approach the sacredness of the Christmas Holiday Season, may every Christian believer remember that Jesus is the reason for the season, not shopping or shop-lifting! A word to the spiritually wise is sufficient: "Leave other people's property alone". Forewarned is foretold. Hence, Christian believers, especially Christian Right Evangelicals, remember: "For God sent not his Son into the world to condemn the world; but that the world through him might be save" (John 3:17). Moreover, there is an awesome penalty and consequence to sin. "He that believeth and is baptized shall be saved; but he that believeth not shall be damned" (Mark 16:16).

Moreover, as we enter this holy holiday season, every voice should be lifted in spiritual praise and adoration for the gift of American democratic institutions, because Americans are better than what is being said and done in the eyes of the world-community. Without a doubt, America has always been the spiritual democratic light set on "Freedom Hill" and with "Lady Liberty's" light shining bright, and above all, we should remember that. America has always understood this scriptural-spiritual credo: "For with the heart man believeth unto righteousness; and with the mouth confession is made unto salvation" (Romans 10:10). Hallelujah! Hallelujah! Hallelujah!

Deception and Confusion

In the beginning, Adam and Eve were perfect in the Spirit of God, but they allowed the spirit of the devil in the body of a snake to beguile and confuse Eve. Subsequently, Eve confused Adam and as a consequence both of them sinned against God. Thus, sin lead to God putting them out of their Heaven on earth: The Garden of Eden (The book of Genesis). In the twenty-first century, political and economic mal-discontentment among some Whites and Republican Party loyalists (especially among Christian Right Evangelicals), has fueled an insatiable desire on the part of some Whites for "White Privilege" policies. But, more importantly, propelled an ungodly male into the Presidency of the greatest social democracy known to humankind.

At one time in Heaven, God faced a similar spiritual problem with Lucifer, a beautiful Angel with melodious sounds. Lucifer utilized perception, deception, and confusion to beguile other angels to believe in him and replace God as their God-head. Hence, God kicked out of Heaven thirty-three percent (1/3) of His Kingdom. This action effectively replaced "I Am" with "He Is" which got rid of the spirit of Lucifer. Now, Lucifer's spirit of evil against God is in the air, going to and fro everywhere, seeking whom he may devour.

God loved the world and humanity so much; that He decided to send His only begotten Son, Jesus the Christ, into the world: "God so loved the world, that he gave his only begotten Son, that whosoever believeth in him should not perish, but have everlasting life" (John 3:16). More importantly, "God sent not his Son into the world to condemn the world; but that the world through him might be saved" (John 3:17). The result of this spiritual action was a new spiritual understanding: "He that believeth and is baptized shall be saved; but he that believeth not shall be damned" (Mark 16:16).

Jesus said, "All that the Father giveth me shall come to me; and him that cometh to me I will in no wise cast out" (John 6:37). Even though Judas, the son of prediction, possessing all sorts of evil came to Jesus; Jesus did not cast him out; yet, Judas still betrayed Jesus for thirty pieces of silver (Love of money) with a love kiss. Christian Right Evangelicals and Republican Party loyalists spiritually understand why we were cast out of God's Garden of Eden: SIN. Just as Judas betrayed Jesus with a kiss, Christian Right Evangelicals and Republican Party Loyalists betrayed America by spiritually embracing an ungodly male with their votes because of their desire for White Privilege.

Cain and Abel, the sons of Adam and Eve, allowed the spirit of the devil to create confusion and envy between them and ended in Cain killing Abel. Cain was asked by God: "Where is Abel thy brother?" And he said, "I know not: Am I my brother's keeper?" "What hast thou done?" God asked him (Genesis 4:9-10). Christian Right Evangelicals and Republican Party Loyalists in the twenty-first century are still asking that same devilish question: "Am I my brother's keeper?" even after America affixed and embraced the most powerfully-spiritually-enlightened document in the history of humankind. We continually fail to live up to its powerful spiritual meaning, and we all know that the road to hell is paved with good intentions, not godly, good deeds. Good intentions are not good enough. Good deeds make the difference. Americans are interdependent upon each other, and we must create our own heaven on earth by spiritually, morally, and intellectually working together in peace and harmony, not societal conflict.

However, we know that Heaven on earth is an impossible task with the spirit of anti-Christ leadership (Only, "I, and I alone can fix-it"). The personal pronoun "I" is always the "I" smack dab in the middle of sIn. "For many deceivers have entered into the world, who confess not that Jesus Christ is come in the flesh" (2 John 1:7).

Righteousness came into the world, and the ungodly crucified it. For, after all, Jesus Christ is the "I" in the middle of "Righteousness." The thirty-three percent of President Trump's Republican Party base in conjunction with the hard-core Christian Right Evangelical supporters, who form his voting base, desire White Privileges. Of course, they appear to be spiritually dead or just might be spiritually confused similar to the angelic third that God kicked out of Heaven. Ungodly, devilish confusion and constant lying are not good strategies or indicators of moral understanding for policy leadership or democratic institution-building governance.

Unfortunately, these individuals are instruments for racial and ethnic divisions in American society, as well as possibly initiating wars. However, there is hope in Jesus Christ for even the worst among us. "And the God of peace shall bruise Satan under your feet shortly. The grace of our Lord Jesus Christ be with you. Amen" (Romans 16:20). In the words of a troubled American, (Rodney King) who was unjustly, brutally and severely beaten by police officers asked this profound question: "Can't we all just get along?" If all Americans can spiritually understand and live by Rodney King's statement, we will truly understand these words of Scriptural inspiration: "For though we walk in the flesh, we do not war after the flesh: for the weapons of warfare are not carnal, but mighty through God to the pulling down of strongholds; casting down imaginations, and every high thing that exalts itself against the knowledge of God, and bringing into captivity every thought to the obedience of Christ; and having in a readiness to revenge all disobedience, when your obedience is fulfilled" (2 Corinthians 10:3-5).

If, as Americans, we could spiritually understand that life is too short to live stupidly; and be in perpetual conflict with each other; so as not to be able to spiritually and morally get along. Then we will understand the Scripture verse "Fools make a mock of sin: but among the righteous there is favour" (Proverbs 19:9). Conflict does not resolve problems between individuals or between nation states. Without a doubt, nations rise and fall, but the Word of God is eternally everlasting. "Heaven and earth shall pass away, but my words shall not pass away" (Matthew 24:35). All nation states need both civilian as well as spiritual laws to be governed by, especially if they are going to achieve internal peace and stability. "For what the law could not do, in that it was weak through the flesh, God sending his own Son in the likeness of sinful flesh, and for sin, condemned sin in the flesh: that the righteousness of the law might be fulfilled in us, who walk not after the flesh, but after the Spirit" (Romans 8:3-4). "There is therefore now no condemnation to them which are in Christ Jesus, who walk not after the flesh, but after the Spirit" (Romans 8:1). America, be Spiritual-Faith-Walkers, because it is spiritually commanded that we must "walk by faith, not by sight." (2 Corinthians 6:7). Selah!

Can President Trump Legitimately Moralize Before The United Nations?

From its inception, America has been a living moral contradiction, because of its spiritual governing documents. Prior to the Preamble and the U.S. Constitution, Pilgrim Americans broke bread with the Indians on Thanksgiving and then slaughtered them on Christmas; now, there are less than one million American Indians in their native land. America has rationalized the virtual extinction of Native American Indians by declaring "Native Americans simply lived on the land; we developed the land, and brought forth a Great Nation."

America's greatness is America's justification for Native American genocide. After virtual extinction of the Indians, America ventured to Africa, collaborated with some African Chieftains who captured their enemies and sold them into slavery. Of course, these circumstances were few and far in-between, because the majority of Blacks who were sold into slavery were captured by European Whites and Arabs who savaged villages with guns only taking the strong and the young, and marched them to the sea sending them to America on slave ships. Would you believe that the Europeans who came to America were running from religious persecution, searching for religious freedom and material fortune? What a bunch of Christian Right Evangelical hypocrites!

America's infrastructure was not built by immigrant labor, but off of the backs of free slave labor. Slavery is America's original sin, and even in the twenty-first century, it gives the world a profound snap-shot of America's moral character. It has rightly been written "Thou shalt not make unto thee any graven image, or any likeness of anything that is in heaven above, or that is in the earth beneath, or that is in the water under the earth: thou shalt not bow down thyself to them, nor serve them: for I the Lord thy God am a jealous God, visiting the iniquity of the fathers upon the children unto the third and fourth generation of them that hate me" (Exodus 20:4-6). Racism is a graven image, because it seeks to make skin-color-God.

Currently, American society is not structurally designed by law to keep Blacks and other minorities in a subservient socio-economic status. Hence, there are no laws on the books to maintain a master-slave system. At the same time, we all understand that morality cannot be legislated; hence, we all know that power corrupts and absolute power corrupts absolutely.

America's Founders wrote profound spiritual governing documents, namely, the Preamble and the U.S. Constitution. But, unfortunately they could not live up to the spiritual tenets of the documents themselves. Land grabs were initiated. Property rights laws were written and instituted to protect the theft of land. Police Constabularies were established to protect Whites from Whites, and ultimately, to checkmate black males (National Anthem Controversy). Even in the twenty-first century, police organizations are still oriented toward protecting white males and their property. Of course, white women are viewed as the property of white males. (Remember the Billy Bush Video Tape.) Now run and tell that!

It has traditionally been said: Moral man, immoral society. However, in the public behavioral antics of President Trump is it now: Moral society, immoral man? Christian Right Evangelicals, please help yourselves as well as President Trump to spiritually understand that faith brings joy, not money (things). "Therefore being justified by faith, we have peace with God through our Lord Jesus Christ: by whom also we have access by faith into this grace wherein we stand, and rejoice in hope of the glory of God" (Romans 5:1-2).

The United Nations was created after World War II (Nuclear Bomb) as a peaceful detriment to war through diplomacy and statesmanship, not bombastic vulgar rhetoric. President Trump's speech before the United Nations Assembly was an embarrassment to the spiritual-moral character of the greatest social democracy the world has ever known. Just because America pays an enormous amount (22%) of the economic cost associated with the peace-keeping activities of the United Nations, that's no reason to insult a member nation-state or threaten military action against a rogue nation-state. Diplomatically, American Presidents should always tell the truth based upon empirical facts. Hence, based upon empirical-verifiable-facts member nation-states should work in harmony with each other toward world peace. Moreover, without moralizing or utilizing intimidation tactics, name-calling insults, and threatening insane military actions. Nuclear weapons are deterrents to war. Everyone knows who America is: The most powerful militaristic nation on planet earth; and at the same time, the most generous and benevolent nation.

Christian Right Evangelical supporters, please remind yourselves, as well as President Trump, that America is a member of the United Nations for the sole purpose of making the world a better, safer place, not to be the world's godlike critic. "Let them alone: they be blind leaders of the blind. And, if the blind lead the blind, both shall fall into the ditch" (Luke 15:14). Christians do not have ditch-digging mentality, because they realize when they dig ditches for their brothers; they may as well dig one for themselves. Amen!

America has an exceptionally immoral President in both words and deeds (actions) who is seeking to moralize to the world (nation-states). And, at the same time, America has lost its democratic moral compass. President Trump's words and deeds have caused America to lose national and international respect as well as the moral high ground among nation-states. America, out of EGO (Edge-God-Out), why allow President Trump to lead the world into a nuclear-war holocaust? Just think: if we see the mushroom cloud; it is already too late. Let's not be stuck on stupid! Moreover, why allow a small mind to destroy a nation-state that has literally nothing, but guns and bombs? It has rightly said: "A mind is a terrible thing to waste" What is North Korea? If America destroys North Korea, what have we destroyed? North Korea is a starving nation-state that literally cannot feed itself; who is seeking respect from other countries, but not first giving respect. America has lived with more hostile nations with nuclear weapons than North Korea. We do not have to name them, because everyone knows who they are. But more importantly, we are living with an immoral President who has dysentery of the mouth. Christian Right Evangelicals, "Take heed, and beware of covetousness: for a man's life consisteth not in the abundance of the things which he possesseth" (Luke 12:15). "Life is more than meat, and the body is more than raiment" (Luke 12:23). Selah!

Black History: Does Race Still Matter?

Black history begins with a positive "Who Am I?" experience. Most importantly, in celebrating Black history month, Blacks must celebrate God, because Blacks were given a distorted conception of God by slave owners. Hence, because of institutional racism the black church has become black society. It was so from the beginning, and it will be so until the end of time. Moreover, slavery and Jim Crowism (suffering) helped Blacks to come to know God as the suffering servant; that is, the God of our forefathers who suffers with His children. "Casting all your care upon him; for he careth for you" (1 Peter 5:7). Now that we know better, we must do better. But, instead of doing better, we have become confused by casting our burdens upon naming and claiming pastors, and hooking and crooking politicians. Christian Ministry should not just be in church houses, but ministry should be exercised in our nine-to-five employments, especially now with such a mentality as that of

President Trump in the White House.

Listed below are five Kingdom-building survival musts, because in the past the black church was not only the house of God; it was also the house of godly direction in civic affairs, educational development, and godly teachings against all mind-altering spirits (alcohol, over-the-counter drugs, and street drugs). Moreover, the black church must take the high ground and declare spiritual warfare against all forces of evil, both internally as well as externally.

(1) Is Racial Identity Important To Millennial Blacks?

If race does not matter to millennial Blacks, it should matter. To be sure, American society has not yet come to a point in its historic struggle with race, whereby, it has overcome the vestiges of slavery and institutional racism. The physical "For White Only" signs have been taken down, but the mental signs are still in the minds of many, many Whites. Without a doubt, it is much more difficult to pull down spiritual mental strongholds than taking down physical signs. Blacks should behold the ungodly results of the Presidential election of 2016, and its implications for the world community. The election of Donald J. Trump to the Office of President was spiritually grounded in notions of White Privilege (institutional racism). President Trump's language style and public policy pronouncements are classic examples of a racist exclusionary mindset. Without a doubt, the 2016 Presidential election was not about jobs, international trade agreements, the "Rust-Belt" or coal miners losing jobs, but the racial tanning of American society (multiculturalism).

(2) Positive and Negative Characteristics of HBCUs!

First of all, one hundred years ago we had over three hundred HBCUs. Today, we have one hundred-three (103). What happened? It is a moral-intellectual imperative that we improve all levels of public schooling (K-12), because social democracy requires an intelligent voting populace. As a matter of fact, far too many twenty-first century black students who attend HBCUs are ill-prepared to do college level work. This was not the situational condition prior to 1964 Civil Rights Acts and the Voting Rights Act of 1965. The positive side of attending an HBCU is that students do have opportunities to participate in procedural activities that enhance intellectual development and leadership skills, including remedial classes for non-proficient students. In fact, there is far too much political chicanery in education at every level, and not enough common sense leadership. Above all, HBCU governing officials must clearly realize that the White House initiative on HBCUs under the Trump Administration appears to be facade window dressing, not policy oriented to strengthened capacity and educational quality.

(3) The Institutional Effects of Racism

First of all, blackness is a part of both one's humanity as well as one's divinity. But, more importantly, blackness is rejected by American society and its institutional structure; therefore, racism is a God problem, not a color problem. God hates racism. Whites as well as Blacks have nothing whatsoever to do with the color of their skin; it is the gift of God. The real question is, how does an individual affirm his/her blackness since it is divine?

(4) The Importance of the Word of God

Understanding the following Scriptural verses will enlighten an individual's life journey, his/her spiritual-emotional stability, as well as his/her Christian walk: "But seek ye first the Kingdom of God, and his righteousness, and all these things shall be added unto you" (Matthew 6:33). Above all, "Be sober, be vigilant; because your adversary the devil, as a roaring lion, walketh about, seeking whom he may devour: whom resist stedfast in the faith, knowing that the same afflictions are accomplished in your brethren that are in the world" (1 Peter 5:8-9). "Submit yourselves therefore to God. Resist the devil, and he will flee from you." (James 4:7). Above all, "Be careful for nothing, but in everything by prayer and supplication with thanksgiving let your requests be known unto God. And the peace of God which passesth all understanding, shall keep your hearts and minds through Christ Jesus" (Philippians 4:6-7). It is sin that divides; it is sin that separates individuals from each other. Yesterday, today, and separatism will only end when Jesus comes back again.

(5) Advice for Young People

Young people must be intellectually taught and must spiritually understand that they come into the world innocent; therefore, individuals must be taught that they are a child of God with a great inheritance. The real question is: What are you going to do with your great inheritance from God? Do not believe all that you read and see over the internet. The greatness instrument of the devil in the twenty-first century just might be technology (the internet) and texting. Individuals must stay grounded in the Word of God, because everything you need to know about life is in a "TEXT" from Genesis to Revelation. Obey the Word; look forward and don't look back. Face your trials and tribulations, and when you get knocked down by life's challenges, pick yourself up, continue to fight, and don't back yourselves into cages that others have built for you. Stay away from mind-altering drugs. "A mind is a terrible thing to waste." Reading is spiritually developmental; therefore, read the Book of Life and not just instagram, face-book, media takeout, and so on. "Blessed is he that readeth, and they that hear the words of this prophecy, and keep those things which are written therein: for the time is at hand" (Revelation 1:3). Spend more money on reading materials (books) than on the vanity of the world. Too many young Blacks cannot read, because they do not read. Black churches are duty-bound-spiritually to reclaim young black men from street gangs, schoolhouse dysfunctional clichés, prisons, dysfunctional behaviors and ungodly life-styles. Above all, black churches must be in the forefront of reestablishing a spiritual-defense-system against moral decadence. Selah.

Racism Either Drives Or Draws

Why does racism exist in the most sophisticated and technological enlightened period of the twenty-first century (2017)? By now, you are probably wondering just what will racism drive or draw an individual to? Racism will either drive an individual insane or draw an individual to evil (the devil); both are negative and have negative consequences. The answer to the why question of racism lays in family socialization, pastoral leadership in Christian Right Evangelical churches, and peer group socialization influences. Radical racial indoctrination occurs, because birds of a feather flock together. Most white Americans are not racists. Only about thirty-three and one third (33 1/3) percent of Whites are radical racists, and other Whites simply go along to get along for social acceptance reasons and fear of being attacked. Forewarned is foretold, because silence is consent. After all, evil is spiritual ignorance of the Creator of all things.

Black Americans are not racially motivated in any way, shape, form, or fashion, even though, some Blacks respond negatively to racism. In fact, Blacks have compassion for, and above all, respect for Whites who are culturally inclusive since, on the other hand, they catch hell from racist Whites. Because of this, Blacks are fearful for themselves as well as for their love ones, because they feel a large percentages of Whites want them to apologize for what blackness represents; therefore, they do not have to ask God for forgiveness for their sinful racism. God hates racism, and "God judgeth the righteous, and God is angry with the wicked every day" (Psalm 7:11). Words of truth and love can overcome words of lies, hatred, and societal discord in the eternal struggle of life and death; that is, God versus the devil. "For the law of the Spirit of life in Christ Jesus hath made me free from the law of sin and death. For what the law could not do, in that it was weak through the flesh, God sending his own Son in the likeness of sinful flesh, and for sin, condemned sin in the flesh: that the righteousness of the law might be fulfilled in us, who walk not after the flesh, but after the Spirit" (Romans 8:2-4).

In pondering the domestic terrorist actions of James Alex Fields in Charlottesville, Virginia, an individual must conclude that racism leads to unadulterated demonic evil and makes an individual a prime candidate for the devil's workshop. "For as he thinketh in his heart, so is he" (Proverbs 23:7). Hence, only demonic evil can motivate an individual to drive 800 miles to use his motor vehicle as a weapon of domestic terrorism; especially when he should have been driving to college preparing to enter his junior year of study.

This is simply an example of Reason versus Passion. Of course, an individual is what he or she thinks and believes, and, therefore, his/her beliefs and words shape his/her actions (destiny). Moreover, lack of spiritual-moral leadership in family environments, Christian churches, and other American cultural institutions produces societal alienation. America, know full well, that the truth will either drive you or draw you, because "...the word of God is quick, and powerful, and sharper than any twoedged sword, piercing to dividing asunder of soul and spirit, and of the joints and marrow, and is a discerner of the thoughts and intents of the heart" (Hebrews 4:12).

America has a president who has, from the beginning, licensed racial and religious hatred, and above all, the destruction of democratic institutions. Throughout the primary season and in the general election, Trump embraced the acquired language of racial hatred. The spiritual-moral failure of President Trump was manifestly made crystal clear and complete with his triangulation moral equivalency comments after the Charlottesville terrorist killing. Confederate symbols are statements of White supremacy and hatred and a war against the Federal Union, not democratic egalitarian inclusion. The role of an American President is to calm the nation in difficult times, but for certain, being President does not change who you are; it only reveals who you are. For those Americans who did not know who Donald J. Trump is, now you truly know beyond a shadow of a doubt precisely who Donald J. Trump truly is: A racial bigot, an ungodly religious bigot, a woman hater, and (undoubtedly) the biggest liar to ever occupy The White House.

If we can say President George Washington never told a lie, then without a doubt, we can say unequivocally that President Donald J. Trump has never told the truth. Since becoming President historical media-tracking has identified at least 2,000 public lies uttered from the President's mouth. This is why "Jesus said to those Jews which believed on him, If ye continue in my word, then are ye my disciples indeed: and ye shall know the truth, and the truth shall make you free" (John 8:31-32). Christian Right Evangelicals, President Donald J. Trump has never been a man of God, but a male in the world. The evidence of his lack of God-consciousness is his own declaratory statement regarding "Two Corinthians." Every Christian has been admonished to "Study to shew thyself approved unto God, a workman that needeth not be ashamed, rightly dividing the word of truth. But shun profane and vain babblings: for they will increase unto more ungodliness" (2 Timothy 2:15-16). "Two Corinthians" is profane and vain babbling.

President Donald J. Trump is the most ungodly, unhinged, despicable, morally-spiritually-challenged-unqualified President who has ever occupied The White House. This is precisely why he is more comfortable in a campaigning-politicking-entertainment mode designed solely to keep his voter base politically solidified, because he is not capable of providing Presidential moral leadership. America's international enemies are laughing; God-fearing Americans are crying and wondering "What's Going On?" And, seemingly President Trump has expanded and totally exposed the racist under-belly of the Republican Party, and at the same time, exposed the religious hypocrisy of Christian Right Evangelicals. President Trump, in conjunction with Christian Right Evangelicals, is licensing racial division and racial hatred. America, let's clearly understand the consequences of the declining moral authority of America in the world community, because President Trump wanted a job that he is intellectually, psychologically, and morally incapable of performing. The U. S. Presidency and Donald J. Trump are spiritual misfits. Christian Right Evangelicals, you are not fooling God, only yourselves, because you cannot cloak your racism in Christianity. God hears all and sees all: "For he saith, I have heard thee in a time accepted, and in the day of salvation have I succoured thee: behold, now is the accepted time; behold, now is the day of salvation" (2 Corinthians 6:2). Get right with God! Selah!

If it must be, it shall be!

To be for the sake of being is not a reason in the greatest social democracy on the face of the earth. One of the greatest poetic writers of our time, Alfred Lord Tennyson, said it best: "Ours not to reason why, ours but to do and die." Tennyson was absolutely correct only about spiritual things because individuals die whether they want to or not. "And as it is appointed unto men once to die, but after this the judgment" (Hebrews 9:27). Judgment is spiritual. "God judgeth the righteous, and God is angry with the wicked every day" (Psalm 7:11). After all, we are in the Age of Trump-Doctrine (TRUMPDOM), and every American must believe "The house of the wicked shall be overthrown: but the tabernacle of the upright shall flourish" (Proverbs 14:12). Apparently, President Trump believes in doing evil for the sake of doing evil simply because of a lack of God consciousness and to establish a New World Order, which in turn, would be disastrous for the world.

Tennyson was absolutely incorrect about flesh-oriented things and the material world. Individuals should never choose to die for immoral reasons or causes—only choose to die for a just cause. It is a personal decision that is only in the heart and mind of the individual who chooses to place his life on the line. Of course, only God can judge individual motive, and this is why an individual can do the right thing from the wrong motive, and that is sin.

America, let's be perfectly clear about why Donald J. Trump was elected President of the greatest social democracy in the world. Coded racist phrases and latent racism elected Trump to The White House, in conjunction, with White backlash because of the election of Barack Obama as a two-term President. Let us be clear about why America's democratic institutions are being assaulted. Make no mistake about it, American social democracy and America's leadership in the free world is being trashed by the Trump Administration. President Trump used coded language to white males and some white females so in order to galvanize their votes, and it was successful.

Currently, America is not imperiled by trade agreements, job losses, or socio-economic-political influences in the free-world. The external threats to America's democratic influence in the world community are Russia, China, North Korea, and Iran. However, there are greater socio-spiritual-internal threats to America's well-being, because it is those threats that produced the election of Donald J. Trump to the Office of President. Christian Right Evangelicals, there are consequences in your vote (chaos, confusion, and misuse of governmental resources). You must now own the societal consequences of your spiritual vote. Christian Right Evangelical Pastoral leaders, God is beseeching you to ". . . by the mercies of God, that ye present your bodies a living sacrifice, holy, acceptable unto God, which is your reasonable service. And be not conformed to this world: but be ye transformed by the renewing of your mind, that ye may prove what is that good, and acceptable, and perfect will of God" (Romans 12:1-2).

By the way, Donald J. Trump emphatically told you that he could not come anywhere near any of these spiritual precepts. And, yet, you still voted for a merciless, confused, uncaring individual who told you; he could "shoot someone on Fifth Avenue, and you would still support him." Hypocrites, hypocrites, and hypocrites! "Thou hypocrite, first cast out the beam that is in thine own eye; and then shalt thou see clearly to cast out the mote out of thy brother's eye" (Matthew 7:5). More importantly, pastoral leaders, preach and espouse the Gospel of Jesus Christ, and above all, preach the truth about race and stop preaching personalized-isms. "Isms" create schisms which are not of God. God hates racism. (An example of this is the story of Miriam and Aaron and their hatred toward the

Ethiopian woman whom Moses married: Numbers 12:1-16). Racism creates insanity, and without a doubt, America has governing insanity going on in The White House. In recent national polling data, it has been empirically documented that the level of racism in American society was underestimated by most God-fearing Americans.

Donald J. Trump told the American people in no uncertain terms the unadulterated truth about himself which was mostly evil. Love is an outward expression of an internal spiritual reality (God). Love is about giving, not self-centered ego-taking. "EGO" is an acronym for "Edge-God-Out." Initially, there were 613 commandments and the "chosen people of God (Israelites)" could not live by them. God condensed them to ten (10), The Ten Commandments, which He gave to Moses on Mt. Sinai, and still most individuals could not live by them.

An ungodly lawyer dealing the power of technicality (lies) asked Jesus a question, tempting Him, saying, "Master, which is the greatest Commandment in the law? Jesus said unto him, Thou shalt love the Lord thy God with all thy heart, and with all thy soul, and with all thy mind. This is the first and great commandment. And the second is like unto it, Thou shalt love thy neighbor as thyself. On these two commandments hang all the law and the prophets"

(Matthew 22:37-40). Christian Right Evangelicals, this is a profound spiritual lesson that President Trump evidently never learned, and Trump certainly does not practice it. Trump's commandment is the "I" syndrome that is the "I" that is smack-dab in the middle of "sIn".

It is, indeed unfortunate; because it seems as though eighty (80%) percent of Christian Right Evangelicals who supported Trump did not learn this spiritual lesson either. Obviously, individuals cannot teach with spiritual fervor that which they do not believe. America, President Trump's leadership behavior suggests that he, indeed, does not know anything about the love of God, love for country, or positive love for self. Moreover, when individuals do not understand this spiritual fact of life, they are already in hell, and their only choice is to create hell for others. America, "In God We Trust," and those who trust in President Trump know full well that he is creating hell in America.

Some white men consistently lied on Hillary Clinton, but absolutely nothing criminal was ever proven (under oath) after numerous congressional investigations and hearings. All of this partisan-political nonsense for White Privilege produced nothing in spite of Republicans being in-charge of both the House and the Senate. But, more importantly, Senators Collins and Murkowski are profound socio-spiritual examples of why America just might need more women in politics rather than fewer. Finally, America, there are two spiritual traits that an individual must possess for God to entrust him/her with a godly mission: "And the Lord said unto Moses, I will do this thing also that thou hast spoken: for thou hast found grace in my sight, and I know thee by name" (Exodus 33:17). God does not know everybody by name. Christian Right Evangelicals, does God know President Donald J. Trump by name? Selah!

The State Of The Union

The State of the Union is spiritually-morally upside-down, because President Donald J. Trump is America's greatest national disaster! If you thought acts of nature (hurricanes, mud slides, floods, wild fires, tornadoes) and individuals driving cars without driver's licenses were disastrous, sorry to inform you, President Trump tops all of these calamities.

February is Black History Month: An historic legacy celebration of great individuals of color from the "S-Hole" Continent of Africa, who were brought to America as free-slave labor to build America's infrastructure. Just to mention a few: Fredrick Douglas, Harriet Tubman, Benjamin Banneker, Mary McCloud Bethune, George Washington Carver, Madame C.J. Walker, Booker T. Washington, Ethel Waters, and Dr. Martin L. King, Jr. Additionally, there is one great American who is white who every black American should always remember and never forget, because only a few white men would have had the spiritual-moral courage to do what President

Lyndon B. Johnson (LBJ) did at that time in America's turbulent history. He orchestrated the passage of the 1964 Civil Rights Act and the 1965 Voting Rights Act. Most importantly, President Johnson instituted a national governmental war on poverty. A lot has been said and will be said about LBJ, but God-fearing individuals give no place to the devil. Trump thinks that he should be enshrined on Mount Rushmore. Yet, on the other hand, there are those who believe that President Lyndon B. Johnson (LBJ) for his contributions to American society in morally-trying-times, his image should be carved on Mount Rushmore. Of course, President Trump is legislatively attempting to undo all of it by making America great again. Oops! I meant to say: "White-Privilege-oriented" again as though it ever stopped being that way.

The State of the Union, when you get right down to it, is divided spiritually and morally along racial/ethnic lines. Simply, because some Whites want White Privilege, while Blacks and other permanent-tan minorities just want to be included. Christian Right Evangelical leadership and Republican Party leadership have given rise to the most spiritually-morally-bankrupt-despicable individual to ever occupy the greatest political leadership position in the world. Moreover, Republican co-conspirators, as well as President Trump, please remember this: "All that glitters is not gold." For certain, we all know that the wheels of justice grind ever so slowly, but ever so fine; and when justice runs its course, as it will, the spiritual concept of all "gones" are not good byes. Instead, they will become the after-shocks of destruction for democratic institutional norms in the form of Spiritual retribution for sin! "Be not deceived: God is not mocked: for whatsoever a man soweth, that shall he also reap" (Galatians 6:7). Christian Right Evangelicals, you spiritually understand, but lack the moral courage to practice what you preach and teach in God's presence.

The Russians do not need to militarily invade America simply because the Russian mentality is already alive and well in the psyche of far too many Americans, especially in some who work in The White House. Beyond a shadow of a doubt, everyone needs to understand this: Corruption corrupts, and absolute power produces absolute corruption. President Trump was a convenient leadership vehicle for a corrupt leadership mentality to come to the forefront and flourish in the Republican Party.

Traditional Republican Party principles of freedom and justice for all was compromised (or corrupted) in 1964 when Republicans embraced The Southern Strategy. Of course, Christian Right Evangelicals have been spiritually corrupted for a long, long time, because of their love of money which, in turn, is the root of all evil (1 Timothy 6:10). The desire of Christian Right Evangelicals for absolute power was transformed into love of money. At the same time, the 11:00 o'clock AM worship hour on Sunday morning is and has been, and, seemingly, will always remain the most racially-segregated hour in American society. "For as he thinketh in his heart, so is he" (Proverbs 23:7). For spiritual understanding, perhaps most Whites fear that a spiritual change might come over them, for "Can two walk together, except they be agreed?" (Amos 3:3).

The Republican Party and Christian Right Evangelicals are proving themselves to be the offspring of Cain, seemingly because, they have made a deal with the devil in all of his earthly glory. As a matter of fact, President Trump became the face of the Birther Movement, and he demanded that President Obama produce his Birth Certificate. What goes around comes around (Karma); and now, the new reality is that the shoe is on the other foot. As a result, because of President Trump's unstable and downright unorthodox leadership-personality-mentality-style, the American people should demand that he take a professional sanity test and the empirical test results be released for public edification.

Christian Right Evangelicals, prior to voting for the "Trumpster," you should have explained the spiritual and moral meaning of social democracy to Donald J. Trump. First of all, every individual work's for himself/herself; therefore the White House staff does not work for you, but they work with you on behalf of the American people. No individual works for another individual in a democratic society. More importantly, no God-fearing individual will give a loyalty oath to become a participant in governmental corruption. Without a doubt, corruption is about motive and so is sin. Individuals simply work with other individuals, not for them, because each individual works for his/her own family. President Trump and like-minded-Republicans; especially, Judge Roy Moore, chattel slavery ended on January 1st, 1863.

In the case of the U.S. Presidency, the President governs (works) on behalf of the country (American people). He hires individuals who are willing to do likewise. For certain, the Office of the Presidency is not intended to be a "private-money-making" business venture that gives a President the power to spiritually-morally-bankrupt the culture as well as democratic institutions for the love of power and money. Maybe this is why President Trump has filed financial bankruptcy four times. Instead of setting moral examples, ethical standards of behavior, and honoring time-honored-proven-traditional standards of human decency, public service and civility, Donald J. Trump has trashed ethical-moral-standards of Presidential conduct. Unfortunately, given his public leadership behavior, he has provided empirical-confirmation- evidence pertaining to who Republicans are: A Political Party of spiritually-morally-confused individuals!

Christian Right Evangelicals, where are your family values and sense of moral conscience? Republican politicians, where is your statesman-like moral conscience concerning Law and Order? Trashing the Federal Bureau of Investigation (FBI), an institution that has protected America from foreign and domestic enemies, is now being trashed to protect an unworthy, immoral, bigoted President who desires to be a dictator of the world's greatest social democracy. Thus, are Devin Nunez and Speaker Paul Ryan moles for a foreign government? "Be not deceived: evil communication corrupt good manners" (1 Corinthians 15:33) Selah!

Subliminal Implanting

Has America been subliminally beguiled by President Donald J. Trump into playing spiritual mind games with our conscience as well as with our democratic institutions? If so, then God have mercy upon the soul of the nation! Beware, America, and "Take heed, and beware of covetousness: for a man's life consisteth not in the abundance of the things which he possesseth" (Luke 12:15). More importantly, Christian Right Evangelicals, "A little that a righteous man hath is better than the riches of many wicked" (Psalm 37:16) because ". . . what shall it profit a man, if he shall gain the whole world, and lose his own soul. Or what shall a man give in exchange for his soul?" (Mark 8:36-37). Christian Right Evangelicals, sin is sin, and there is no such thing as a little sin and a big sin. God hates all sins, so stop picking and choosing sin(s) for God because ". . . all have sinned, and come short of the glory of God" (Romans 3:23).

Moreover, know this: "God judgeth the righteous, and God is angry with the wicked every day" (Psalm 7:11). Christian Right

Evangelicals, God hates a lying tongue and Scripture teaches us to "Lay hands suddenly on no man, neither be a partaker of other men's sins: Keep thyself pure" (1 Timothy 5:22). Therefore, Christian Right Evangelicals, "I charge thee before God, and the Lord Jesus Christ, and the elect angels, that thou observe these things without preferring one before another, doing nothing by partially" (1 Timothy 5:21). Politics engenders strange bed-fellows. America, especially Christian Right Evangelicals, get out of the bed with President Donald J. Trump, because your souls are in question! Just a reminder: you are not immortal on planet earth, but you will be judged for soul-residency immortality in Heaven or hell. "And as it is appointed unto men once to die: but after this the judgment" (Hebrews 9:27).

Once upon a time, we had a President who was a peacemaker, and he declared that America needed a Big "Peace-keeping" Stick, but America needed to know how to walk spiritually soft with that Big Stick (President Theodore Roosevelt). Now, we have a fool-hearty President (President Donald J. Trump) who does not understand the spirituality of the "Big Stick" principle, because he desires to place the 'Big Stick" in a parade designed solely to glorify him. "Fools make a mock at sin: but among the righteous there is favor" (Proverbs 14:9).

America's greatness is not in its military arsenal. America's greatness is in the Preamble and the U.S. Constitution: "We hold these Truths to be self-evident, that all Men are created equal, that they are endowed by their Creator with certain unalienable Rights, that among these are Life, Liberty, and the Pursuit of Happiness." The words inscribed upon the Statute of Liberty tell the whole truth about America's greatness: "Give me your tired, your poor, your huddled masses yearning to be free, the wretched refuse of teeming shore. Send these, the homeless tempest-tossed to me, I lift my lamp beside the golden door!"

Christian Right Evangelicals, you should have spiritually helped President Trump understand that you cannot kill the truth with a little lie or a big fat lie. The truth creates its own energy. A lie runs on borrowed energy. In short, you cannot kill a good, spiritual idea. President Trump, in conjunction with some conservatives, is boldly attempting to make lying telling the truth by declaring that the truth is "Fake News." Is America losing her soul? The so-called conservative-oriented sector of American society desires to institutionalize lying as fact-based truth (reality) or alternative facts Syndrome.

Native Americans did not lie when they declared "White man speaks with fork tongue." On the other hand, the so called liberal sector of

American society desires to institutionalize sin as an issue of Civil Rights. Sin is about free-will choice(s). Confusion is of the devil, "For God is not the author of confusion, but of peace, as in all churches of the saints" (1 Corinthians 14:33). Life is not about extremes. Life is about the in-between, and at the center of all things is the reality of God (Truth).

No sensible, sane-minded American ever thought that, potentially, one individual could literally, potentially destroy America's democratic institutional fabric. Behold the times are changing. Moreover, it was universally thought that we were too sophisticated to allow dictatorship to emerge in American culture, since we rejected the idea of an anointed King: The Revolutionary War. Of course, in the twenty-first century, Putin has been able to accomplish the task, so just maybe it only takes one dictatorial-minded man to undermine democracy. President Trump has in no uncertain terms proven that even in America it can possibly be done; especially with spiritually like-minded individuals whose mindset is White Privilege (Anti-Minorities).

Thirty-three percent of Americans lost their souls (minds) when they accepted the spiritual-moral precepts of a lying, racist, xenophobic, sexist individual who has reneged on business debts and will not pay his fair share of taxes. Shame! Shame! Shame! Why?

And, of course, President Trump over-utilizes the privilege of taxpayer dollars. Down through the ages, White working-class individuals have been sold a "false-bill-of-goods"; that is, if you are White, you should be successful, because the American Dream is a "White Dream": White Privilege. Hence, if you are not successful, it must be because of permanent-tan minorities who are your enemies, and they have taken control over what rightfully belongs to you.

Sadly, though, the consequences of this socio-cultural insanity are individuals who will purchase an assault rifle and destroy innocent lives in public schools and public places. Hatred knows no skin color. Consequently, the system uses God as an acronym: Guns-Oil-Drugs. This socio-economic trinity generates money for the rich class. However, what White working-class individuals do not spiritually understand is that rich white men outsourced (shipped) your jobs overseas to permanent-tan individuals in foreign countries for cheap labor (profits), not American minorities. Hence, when an advanced civilized society makes money their god, it morally declines. America is on the edge of potential internal-civil-discord conflict, because of special prosecutor Mueller's investigation of Russian meddling in the 2016 Presidential election.

When the final report is released, and it implicates President Trump, as well as, members of his immediate family for conspiracy to undermine America's social democracy, all hell is going to break loose (civil-strife). The Presidency of Donald J. Trump has proven beyond a shadow of any reasonable doubt that all Presidential candidates should be background vetted by the FBI, the CIA, as well as mental health professionals. If such a security-background-legal process had been in place, Donald J. Trump would have been immediately disqualified to seek any public office, even that of a public-dog-catcher. He has and will always be qualified to be a billionaire simply, because of his ability to hook-crook with foreign money (other people's money). As it is written, "for the love of money is the root of all evil." America, lest we forget: "A good name is rather to be chosen than great riches, and loving favor rather than silver or gold" (Proverbs 22:1). Selah!

Good Men Take A Moral Stand

Every American should truly understand that we are in a monumental spiritual-moral crisis, whereby, too many Americans are attempting to make wrong, right and make it work. This approach to harmonious living with God, others, and nature is a spiritually disastrous formula for any civilized democratic society. Listening is a godly quality, and a refusal to listen to sound spiritual doctrines invariably leads to a loss of spiritual hearing and moral understanding. "Therefore to him that knoweth to do good, and doeth it not, to him it is sin" (James 4:17).

American society is at a spiritual-moral-line-of-demarcation, and it appears as though we are about to cross over into oblivion, especially as it relates to Presidential political leadership. If so-called Christian Right Evangelicals do not come to their spiritual-faithful-teachings sense based upon Biblical doctrines, we could lose it all.

Currently, too many Christian Right Evangelicals have itchy ears and are now chasing after fables and false divisive doctrines. "For the time will come when they will not endure sound doctrine; but after their own lusts shall they heap to themselves teachers, having itching ears; and they shall turn away their ears from the truth, and shall be turned unto fables" (2 Timothy 4:3-4). This is already the circumstance with President Trump. Christian Right Evangelicals do not allow this to happen to you.

There are some things that should not be legislated. This is why God gave us free-will choice. Moreover, God has already legislated morality in "The Ten Commandments". Without a doubt, The Ten Commandments are all the laws we need. Unfortunately, most individuals cannot live by them; thus, they look to thousands of man-made laws instead.

It has become vividly clear, given the Russian hacking of the 2016 Presidential election that America needs to elect more god-fearing women to political offices. Why? It seems as though in the twenty-first century, women appear to be more conscience-oriented and spiritually sensitive to the will of God that tells us to love one another. Too many men have abandoned the fortitude to embrace the will of God, but have seemingly embraced their own selfish wills for the love of power, money, and sex (PMS). Seemingly, too many men have lost their praise for God's glory, but have glorified themselves in the love of self, power, money, and sex. PMS (emotional-thinking) among women only lasts for one or two days. On the other hand PMS, that is emotional thinking among most men, appears to be a permanent state of being, not a temporary condition. By the way, in case you did not know it, (PMS) emotional thinking among men is grounded in the love of power, money, and sex, not the love of God the embodiment of truth.

Evidently, too many Republican men in political power positions are dealing with Trumpian-style feelings rather than sound spiritual doctrine based upon spiritual-moral facts and truths. They have an ungodly love affair with alternative facts (lies). Going along to get along is a hellish condition that is attempting to make wrong, right and right, wrong. These so-called political leaders are tearing down the spiritual-moral tenets of American social democracy and its institutions. Consequently, American society is experiencing a monumental disastrous spiritual-moral crisis of Presidential leadership fueled by spiritually hellish Christian Right Evangelicals. Everyone who says, "Lord, Lord," does not have LORD in them. "There is therefore now no condemnation to them which are in Christ Jesus, who walk not after the flesh, but after the Spirit. For the law of the Spirit of life in Christ Jesus hath made me free from the law of sin and death. For what the law could not do, in that it was weak through the flesh, God sending his own Son in the likeness of sinful flesh, and for sin, condemned sin in the flesh: that the righteousness of the law might be fulfilled in us, who walk not after the flesh, but after the Spirit"(Romans 8:1-4).

Christian Right Evangelicals, you need to learn godly patience and spiritual discipline according to the Word of God. "For we are saved by hope: but hope that is seen is not hope: for what a man seeth, why doth he yet hope for?" (Greed, Envy, and Jealousy). "But if we hope for that we see not, then do we with patience wait for it" (Romans 8:24-25). Christian Right Evangelicals, you must first understand and accept sound, spiritual doctrine to receive this spiritual message. Moreover, please share this spiritual message with President Donald J. Trump. All hope is not godly hope. Some hope is of physical sight and vanity of the flesh. President Trump's false hope that FBI Director Comey could see his way clear to cease investigating General Flynn is sinful, false hope. God-fearing American taxpayers are hoping for the opportunity to review President Trump's income tax returns because his tax returns will reveal precisely who he truly serves: America, himself, Russia, China, Saudi Arabia, or other foreign nations.

America, know full well that "We are saved by hope: but hope that is seen is not hope: for what a man seeth, why doth he yet hope for?

But if we hope for that we see not, then do we with patience wait for it" (Romans 8:24-25). President Trump supporters, if you can see it with your physical sight, it is truly vanity of the flesh, not spiritual hope.

There are demonic, fleshy forces (Power, Money, and Sex) that love operating in high places, that are diligently working against the Holy Bible as well as America's sacred Preamble to the U.S. Constitution: "We hold these Truths to be self-evident, that all men are created equal . . ." All Americans understand this Word of God: "What shall we then say to these things? If God be for us, who can be against us?" (Romans 8:31). More importantly, "We know that all things work together for good to them that love God, to them who are the called according to his purpose" (Romans 8:28). President Trump, Christian Right Evangelicals, Republican and Democratic Partisans, and middle-of-the-road Independents who pledge their loyalty to sinful flesh and man-made sinful institutions above God's unrestricted love for us, please understand this Word of God: "For I am persuaded, that neither death, nor life, nor angels, nor principalities, nor powers, nor things to come, nor height, nor death, nor any other creature, shall be able to separate us from the love God, which is in Christ Jesus our Lord" (Romans 8:38-39). Selah!

Man Is God's Glory!

A man's willingness to glorify God is what makes him a man of God, not a male of the world; hence, a worldly male can easily be persuaded to become a lifetime, card-carrying member of the devil's workshop. And "We know that all things work together for good to them that love God, to them who are the called according to his purpose" (Romans 8:28). Every man, every woman, and every child should be a person of God. However, "the called" are Christian pastors whom God has called to shepherd souls. By the way, we can only judge a tree (Pastors) by the fruit it bears. "But as it is written, Eye hath not seen, nor ear heard, neither have entered into the heart of man, the things which God hath prepared for them that love him" (1 Corinthians 2:8-9).

The Republican Party, in conjunction with the Christian Right Evangelical church community, took a page out of the devil's playbook when they overwhelmingly voted for a chronic-habitual liar and a dehumanizer of women, "who are a man's glory": "For a man indeed ought not to cover his head, forasmuch as he is the image and glory of God: but the woman is the glory of the man" (1 Corinthians 11:7-8). Therefore, men should love, protect, and teach women spiritual and moral precepts/concepts. Women should always support men in their desire to have a spiritual relationship with God, and at the same time, teach children the social graces of American society utilizing the truth of God (Bible).

Trump voters, "Professing themselves to be wise, became fools" (Romans 1:22). Every Christian knows that "Fools make a mock at sin: but among the righteous there is favor" (Proverbs 14:9). Has America lost her relationship with God? Perhaps, this is why Christian Right Evangelicals and the Republican Party, in conjunction with a few confused Americans, elected the biggest hypocrite in America's history! With all of the class-act good men seeking the Republican Party's Presidential nomination, why choose an ungodly man such as Donald J. Trump who by his own public testimony, social behavior, and sexist attitudes toward women has proven to be America's greatest national disaster?

America, let's be honest with ourselves. The 2016 Presidential election was not about jobs, trade agreements, wages, healthcare, draining the swamp, or any other socio-economic variable. The 2016 Presidential election was about racial identity and White Privilege

(Alt-Right-Ism). An "ISM" is a schism and schisms divide. Radicalized racial thinking will either drive you or draw you to evil or good. Know this, America, an ungodly man such as President Trump can bring America to nuclear Armageddon. This every American clearly understands by President Trump's own public tweets and public declarations/pronouncements concerning war. For example: if we have nuclear weapons, why can't we use them? To be sure, President Trump does not spiritually-morally understand that America has nuclear weapons as a deterrent to war, not because America desires to wage war and kill millions of innocent civilians.

In a People Magazine interview in 1998, Donald J. Trump emphatically stated: "If I were to run, I'd run as a Republican. They're the dumbest group of voters in the country. They believe anything on Fox News. I could lie and they'd still eat it up. I bet my numbers would be terrific." Donald J. Trump for once in his life did not lie. In fact, he proved his point. And, we know that Christian Right Evangelicals and Republican voters did not vote for Donald J. Trump (the male). Of course, he told them that he was not a man of God through words and deeds. President Trump was simply a convenient vehicle to perpetuate White Privilege (Alt-Right-Ism).

Republican Party Voters and Christian Right Evangelicals knew they were voting for a carnal-minded male to be President, because he told them exactly who he was. But, what they did not understand is this Scripture: "For to be carnally minded is death; but to be spiritually minded is life and peace. Because the carnal mind is enmity against God: for it is not subject to the law of God, neither indeed can be. So then they that are in the flesh cannot please God" (Romans 8:6-8). Now America is reaping the whirlwind of "Trumpism," and it is written, "You reap what you sow." "For he that soweth to his flesh shall of the flesh reap corruption; but he that soweth to the Spirit shall of the Spirit reap life everlasting. And let us not be weary in well doing: for in due season we shall reap, if we faint not" (Galatians 6:8-9).

What makes a male a Man of God rather than a Male of the World is a spiritual understanding of the four-fold foundation given by God to Adam and Eve in the Garden of Eden: "And God said, Let us make man in our own image, after our likeness . . . So God created man in his own image, in the image of God created he him; male and female created he them . . . And God blessed them, and God said unto them, Be fruitful, and multiply, and replenish the earth, and subdue it" (Genesis 1:26-28). When you are a male of the world you have indeed chosen to become a card-carrying member of the devil's workshop. No doubt about it, the devil is the prince of this world (John 14:30). Therefore, the eternal spiritual question is: "Who is on the Lord's side?"

Individuals are defined by the quality of interpersonal relationships that they have with others based upon their personal relationship with God and not material possessions. Thus, it is written "For what shall it profit a man, if he shall gain the whole world, and lose his own soul?" (Mark 8:36). Physical bodies return to the earth (dirt), but the soul does not die. "And fear not them which kill the body, but are not able to kill the soul: but rather fear him which is able to destroy both soul and body in hell" (Matthew 10:28). When a man (any individual) lacks God-consciousness, he makes choices as though physical life is all there is, yet, in reality, this life is just an introduction to eternity.

President Trump lies perpetually because he does not know "He that hath clean hands, and a pure heart; who hath not lifted up his soul unto vanity, nor sworn deceitfully. He shall receive the blessing from the Lord, and the righteousness from the God of his salvation" (Psalm 24:4-5). America, a real man spiritually understands that if another man gives up his life for all men then he ought to be able to love and serve other men (individuals) in Jesus' name, not himself. And, "to God be the Glory" because ". . . God commendeth his love toward us, in that, while we were yet sinners, Christ died for us" (Romans 5:8). President Trump is a bold hypocrite, and therefore, cannot understand these spiritual words of inspiration (apparently), because he does not have a spiritual relationship with God. This might be why he speaks disparagingly about other human beings! Selah.

God Is The Designer Of Family

God has family on His mind; because the first institution God created was family, not the church. Therefore, the spiritual cornerstone of family is the four-fold spiritual foundation for godly living. "God created man in his own image, in the image of God created he him, male and female created he them. And God blessed them, and God said unto to them, Be fruitful, and multiply, and replenish the earth, and subdue it, and have dominion..." (Genesis 1:26-28). In His command, God did not say have an abortion, nor did God intend same-sex marriage. Let me tell you why. First of all, ". . . it is appointed unto men once to die, but after this the judgment" (Hebrews: 9:27). Second, "Lo, children are an heritage of the Lord, and the fruit of the womb is his reward" (Psalm 127:3). Now, let me tell you why God did not ordain or sanction same-sex- marriage.

Family is a spiritual unit, not an economic unit, even though every family has economic functions and obligations (food, shelter, and clothing). However, your family cannot function as an economic unit whereby you are fighting over money, because fighting is about physical competition rather than spiritual cooperation, and above all, competition creates conflict situations. Here's what the Bible says about individual and family living: "Seek ye first the Kingdom of God, and his righteousness; and all these things shall be added unto you. Take therefore no thought for the morrow: for the morrow shall take thought for the things of itself. Sufficient unto the day is the evil thereof" (Matthew 6:33-34). Jesus was teaching His disciples how not to worry about things that you have no control over.

What Happened To The Black Family? Prior to the Civil Rights Act of 1964 and the Voting Rights Act of 1965, eighty percent of all black children born in America were born into two parent households. What happened? Presently, in the twenty-first century the script has flipped. Now, only twenty percent of the black children born in America are born into two-parent households. Couple this fact with the phenomenon of children raising children and what you have is a recipe for disaster. We have left two generations of young Blacks behind primarily for these reasons:

1. A paradigm shift from living from the inside to the outside. Individuals who play outside too long become confused about the

meaning of life. Internal values versus external values.

2. Blacks, just like their White counterparts have become overly materialistic and vulgarly "vanity-oriented"; constantly seeking to maximize the pleasure principle. Prior to 1964 and 1965 Blacks were more internal and spiritual, not materialistic.

3. Blacks have abandoned the notion of faithful church attendance for many and varied reasons, and as a result, the Black community is in moral spiritual decline.

4. Lack of understanding of money. Money is a seed. Money is a tool and it must be used as a tool, not as a fool. Hence, be careful what you plant your seed (s) into!

5. The five wealthiest white families in America have more wealth/money than all forty million blacks in America. Why?

Life is about setting priorities. Priorities are values, and when your priorities are misdirected life becomes a ball of confusion. Selah!

Christian Leadership

There is a time-honored question that individuals have asked throughout the ages: Are leaders born or are leaders made? My purpose in raising the question is not to convince the audience one way or the other. My desire is simply that every person under the sound of my voice allows his or her own conscience to convict them. Here's what the Word of God says: "Even everyone that is called by my name: for I have created him for my glory, I have formed him; yea, I have made him" (Isaiah 43:7). Moreover, "This people have I formed for myself: they shall show forth my praise" (Isaiah 43:21).

Leadership and followership are flip-sides of the same coin. You can't lead if you do not know how to follow. Everyone cannot be a Martin L. King, but you can be a Jessie Jackson, an Al Sharpton, a Andrew Young, or a Ralph Abernathy. Moreover, "Whereby are given unto us exceeding great and precious promises: that by these ye might be partakers of the divine nature, having escaped the corruption that is in the world through lust" (2 Peter 1:4). We need laws, but especially leaders. This is why the Book of Joshua declares "This book of the law shall not depart out of thy mouth: but thou shalt meditate therein day and night, that thou mayest observe to do according to all that is written therein: for then thou shalt make thy way prosperous, and then thou shalt have good success" (Joshua 1:9).

A spiritual leader must always allow God to instruct him through conscience and Holy Scriptures (Word of God). God tells us in His Word "I will instruct thee and teach thee in the way which thou shalt go: I will guide thee with mine eye" (Psalm 32:8). Of course, God's eye is a spiritual eye. "All scripture is given by inspiration of God, and profitable for doctrine, for reproof, for correction, for instruction in righteousness: that the man of God may be perfect, thoroughly furnished unto all good works" (2 Timothy 3:16-17). Every leader must always give his testimony, because "Thy testimonies also are my delight and my counselors" (Psalm 119:24). And this is for the young people in the audience: "Wherewithal shall a young man cleanse his way? By taking heed thereto according to thy word" (Psalm 119:9).

Without a doubt, an individual must be born before he or she can be made. Christian leadership is of God and must be solely defined according to Biblical precepts as well as the principles of God. On, the other hand, secular leadership is of the world and more often than not oriented toward money-making principles and secularism rather than the principles of God; therefore, Christian leadership is about setting examples and precepts. Jesus was the Master-Teacher sent from God to establish eternal examples and precepts. For example: Jesus washing the disciples' feet (John 13:14-15). The disciples were concerned about power and privilege, but Jesus was concerned about love and service. The power is in loving and serving others.

The spiritual-moral walls of American society have been torn down. The glaring twenty-first century example of this spiritual fact is the election of Donald John Trump to the Presidency primarily by so-called Christian Right Evangelicals. Eighty-one percent (81%) of the Evangelicals, who voted, voted for Trump after seeing and hearing him in his own words and actions. If this is not ungodliness, I do not know what is, because the Word of God explicitly warns us to: "Lay hands suddenly on no man, neither be a partaker of other men's sins: Keep thyself pure" (1 Timothy 5:22).

If America is going to survive and thrive, Christian churches must come together in spiritual unity under the leadership authority of God, Jesus, and the Holy Spirit.

Collection Plate Christianity

The purpose of Christianity is reflected in the following: "This is a faithful saying, and worthy of all acceptation, that Christ Jesus came into the world to save sinners" (1 Timothy 1:15). Above all, "For God so loved the world, that he gave his only begotten Son, that whosoever believeth in him should not perish, but have everlasting life" (John 3:16). More importantly, "For God sent not his Son into the world to condemn the world; but that the world through him might be saved" (John 3:17). Here's what the "MIGHT" is about: It's all about your personal FAITH, because there is no equivocation with God or God's Word. All of LIFE is about personal FAITH in God and God's Scriptures of inspiration. "All scripture is given by inspiration of God, and is profitable for doctrine, for reproof, for correction, for instruction in righteousness: that the man of God be perfect, thoroughly furnished unto all good works" (2 Timothy 3:16-17). Of course, most individuals know good works when they see them. Faithful Christians know ". . . that all things work together for good to them that love God, to them who are the called according to his purpose" (Romans 8:28).

For certain, it was not the spiritual purpose of Jesus Christ to establish a "Collection Plate Religion." In fact, Jesus chased money changers out of the Temple. Jesus' purpose was spiritual reconciliation of individuals unto God as well as spiritual reconciliation of individuals unto each other. Remember Cain killed his own brother, and when confronted by God lied about the killing, and then asked God: "Am I my brother's keeper?" (Genesis 4:9).

Jesus' objective was to build the spiritual church in the hearts and minds of individuals through faith. This is why Jesus asked individuals this question: "Whom do men say that I the Son of Man am? And they said, Some say John the Baptist; and others, Elijah; but still others, Jeremiah, or one of the prophets. He said to them, But who do you say that I am? And Simon Peter answered and said, Thou art the Christ, the Son of the living God. And Jesus answered and said to him, Blessed are you, Simon Bar-jona, because flesh and blood did not reveal this to you, but my Father who is in heaven. And I also say to you that you are Peter, and upon this rock I will build my church: and the gates of Hell shall not prevail against it" (Matthew 16:13-19). The Christian church was built on FAITH.

Men build physical churches, because they are physical beings who have physical needs; not gods, even though spiritually they are called to be Christ-like (Christians). Too many Christian pastors have embraced physical church buildings rather than building Christian families through faith. Christianity is a family religion, and this is why Joshua could declare "And if it seem evil unto you to serve the Lord, choose you this day whom ye will serve; whether the gods which your fathers served that were on the other side of the flood, or the gods of the Amorites, in whose land we dwell: but as for me and my house, we will serve the Lord" (Joshua 24:15). Joshua's confession is about family prayers and worship, because the family that prays and worships God together stays together. It's all about family. Christianity is a family religion because "Can two walk together, except they be agreed?" (Amos 3:3). In Christianity, we are eternal brothers and sisters in Christ.

As a matter of fact, ". . . every house is builded by some man; but he that built all things is God" (Hebrews 3:4). And, of course, "Except the Lord build the house, they labour in vain that build it: except the Lord keep the city, the watchman waketh but in vain" (Psalm: 129:1). Nevertheless, as Christians, we should never forget this faithful saying. Individuals must give monetarily in a spiritual manner for physical churches to exist. "For by grace are ye saved through faith;

and that not of yourselves: it is the gift of God: not works, lest any man should boast. For we are his workmanship, created in Christ Jesus unto good works, which God hath before ordained that we should walk in them" (Ephesians 2:8-10). It is grace not works, even though we must work simply, because work is the gift of God. And, as we seek to do the will and work of God in the vineyard of life, we will be troubled on every side, but not in distress: "But, God."

We will be persecuted by both so-called friends as well as professional enemies alike: "But, God." Sometimes we will be wounded and bloodied, but yet unbowed: "But, God." As Christians, we will be down-trodden, but not beaten down: "But, God." And, as Christians, we will be cast down, but not destroyed and bloodied: "But, God." Faithful Christians, know that the race is not given to the swift or faint of heart, but to those who endure to the end, because Christians understand that Jesus desires you to: "Come unto me, all ye that labour and are heavy laden and I will give you rest. Take my yoke upon you, and learn of me; for I am meek and lowly in heart: and ye shall find rest unto your souls. For my yoke is easy, and my burden is light" (Matthew 11:28).

The Church is a spiritual fortress from the "wiles of the devil," not an economic institution, even though it has economic functions. "He hath shewed thee, O man, what is good; and what doth the Lord require of thee, but to do justly, and to love mercy, and to walk humbly with thy God?" (Micah 6:8). Therefore, the church exists to reinforce in our conscience what God requires of us through faith. Moreover, it is by faith that we come to full spiritual knowledge in our hearts and minds that Jesus died for us, that His precious blood was shed for us, and on the third day; He rose from the dead with all power in His hands. Now, He is at the right hand of God preparing a place for us, and above all, making intercession for us. Therefore, "I will say of the Lord, He is my refuge and my fortress: my God; in him will I trust" (Psalm 91:2). After all is said and done, this is why every Christian can say, "Surely goodness and mercy shall follow me all the days of my life: and I will dwell in the house of the Lord forever" (Psalm 23:6).

Black society is the black church, and this is precisely why no pastoral leader should ever take any more from a local church congregation than any hard-working parishioner of the congregation. Extravagant pastoral affluence is ungodly and vulgar. Entering the House of the Lord ought to be a delight; it was for King David a man after God's own heart who said: "I was glad when they said unto me, Let us go into the house of the Lord" (Psalm 122:1). Selah!

Educational Development is the Key to the American Dream

Minority children, especially black children are caught in a circus-like-quagmire of dysfunctional educational environments: home, church, and school. It's time-out time. Family environment and single-parent-family households are serious societal problems. We have had some strange and contestable variables operating in the black community for decades. For those of you who are not familiar with the statistical concept variable, a variable is the property characteristic of a unit of analyses which takes on different values across different units of analyses. Strange wouldn't you say?

At the federal educational leadership level, U. S. Department of Education, there is not a whole-hearted-commitment to public school education. The leadership mentality of the Secretary of Education is not totally committed to public schools. The notion of private Charter schools is the focus. It is the desire of the Trump Administration to use federal taxpayer dollars to allow suburban White families to purchase a private school education with taxpayer dollars. It goes without saying that large urban school districts are primarily Black and Brown, for example, the Houston ISD (HISD) is ninety percent minority, and only ten-percent White. White flight and primarily suburban school districts are primarily designed to educate affluent white children. HISD is used in the context of talking about the systematic efforts on the part of conservative whites to maintain a system of segregated public education: thereby averting implementing the 1954 Supreme Court decision: Brown versus Board of Education.

Of course, one educational size does not fit all. Home is the first and the last school, and therefore, in too many black families educational values are not top priorities in the twenty-first century. We all know that too many black children are growing up in dysfunctional family environments (ghettos); whereby just physically surviving is the priority, not intellectual development. Moreover, we need black churches to "step-up and reach-out" and spiritually begin to foster nuclear family unifying behavioral relationship patterns by taking the church to the ghetto (Great

Commission). By the way, there are a lot of churches in existence in the ghettos, but in many instances the leadership is not oriented toward loving and serving in the ghettos. Consequently, too many black children are being secularly nurtured in family environments that rarely, if ever, attend church primarily, because their parents do not attend.

We know that children who frequently attend church are more likely to be academically successful in school. Children who frequently attend church are spiritually bent toward internal self-discipline, not just external environmental authority control (policing). Moreover, children who frequently attend church are spiritually aware of God's Word, precepts, and principles. "Blessed is he that readeth, and they that hear the words of this prophecy, and keep those things which are written therein: for the time is at hand" (Revelation 4:1). But, more importantly, ". . . faith cometh by hearing, and hearing by the word of God" (Romans 10:17).

The Houston Independent School District under the state's new evaluation system for school districts recently received low grades on key educational domains. For example: fourteen (14) schools received "F's" on all domains, and seventy-eight (78) schools received "D's" and "F's" on all domains: reading, math, science, and social studies. Overall, HISD earned a "C" for student achievement on the STAAR test. The STAAR test is an assessment tool that measures student proficiency and achievement in core subject areas: This is a report card that HISD did not want parents or the general public to see. HISD is petrified by TEA's letter evaluation grading system of a school district's performance on the STAAR test: State of Texas Assessments of Academic Readiness. Thus, STAAR measures student academic readiness in Math, Writing, Science, and Social Studies. HISD officials feared that such a letter grading system would harm community-parental-morale. Some educators argued that the new letter grading system relies too heavily on standardized tests. Yet, most teachers teach the test rather than teaching children how to listen to learn, and above all, learn how to analytically think. Motto: "Listen to learn and learn to listen". Listening is a godly quality. Christian Right Evangelicals, please tell President Trump!

What children who come from ghetto environments need is:
To be taught reading skills through phonics.
To be taught mathematical skills by learning their time tables.
To be taught writing skills through repetition, repetition, and more repetition.

What public school educators are doing now is absolutely not working, and above all, has had disastrous developmental consequences. If you do not believe me, check out the grades HISD received from the Texas Education Agency (TEA) the state oversight agency. Unfortunately, in their failure and being told that they are failures, many young people are joining gangs and using drugs to prove to themselves; that they are worthy and are socially acceptable. This is precisely why black children need in the worst way spiritual-moral-instruction in their schools and everyday environments. This would help with discipline and social behavioral problems in public schools.

In the past, Wheatley High School was one of Houston's oldest, most prestigious, and highly competitive educational institutions. For example: the likes of Commissioner El Franco Lee, Congresswoman Barbara Jordan, Congressman Mickey Leland, and Bishop I. V. Hilliard are laureates of Wheatley high school. There are many, many others I could name, but the list is too long to give honor to all who deserve honor. Today, Wheatley is in academic decline and has fallen on difficult times, because of a mixture of leadership and academic performance reasons. Former HISD superintendent, Terry Greer, called schools in the inner-city of Houston an educational desert.

Recently, I met with a group of concerned Wheatley graduates. This concerned group of Wheatley graduates, concerned citizens, and many are professional educators, call themselves "Restoring the Wildcat Spirit at 90." Their objectives are as follows: (1) Assist in helping Wheatley improve its accountability rating; (2) Assist in improving post-secondary readiness; (3) Improve the graduation rates; (4) Assist in closing the performance gaps by helping to improve student reading levels, because seventy-five percent (75%) of the students are reading below grade level; and (5) Assist the administration in improving its vision and mission statements. Even though the ethnic make-up of the feeder community surrounding Wheatley has changed, the teaching strategies, learning developmental strategies, and above all, curriculum remain the same. It's not rocket science. Change administrative approaches, teaching strategies, and instructional strategies/approaches to meet the twenty-first century demands of ethnic diversity.

Within the black community, we have unusually talented and gifted professional educators, such as Dr. Rod Paige, former HISD Superintendent and former U. S. Secretary of Education, Dr. Lillian Poats (Texas Southern University), and Dr. James Cunningham (Texas Southern University), who need to be a part of this process. TEA, in conjunction with the Governor's office, should establish a research-based blue-ribbon committee to establish performance-based initiatives on "How best to educate children in a technologically-oriented society, as well as, one that is ethnically diverse." How has HISD adjusted to these environmental school multi-cultural ethnic changes? Professionally, they consulted with former HISD Superintendent Dr. Rod Paige concerning student performance, and after reading his seminal work on closing the "Black-White Achievement Gap," they concluded that student performance is directly linked to administrative leadership management. Moreover, TEA's evaluation of HISD is proof positive. As a result, HISD must enlist the research and development services of Texas Southern University (TSU), University of Houston UHC, and Rice universities in crafting strategies on "how best to educate minority children especially in a school district that is minority-majority". In fact, urban school districts across America might want to adopt a similar public school approach. Selah!

A Clear Present, Past, And Future Danger

Government officials who cannot and will not protect school-age children, who are the nation's future, cannot protect the nation. The obvious question is: Why does this circumstance exist? There is a cause and effect consequence to actions as well as in actions. The spiritual mis-interpretation of the Second Amendment by Christian Right Evangelicals and the Republican Party is helping to exacerbate the issue of public school violence, because of easy access to guns (Weapons of War).

Since the first public school shooting on April 20th, 1999 at Columbine High School (Columbine, Colorado), America has had 270 such public school shootings. Unfortunately, these public school shootings have become an American spiritual-moral tragedy. The National Rifle Association (NRA), The Republican Party, and so-called Christian Right Evangelicals must, therefore, shoulder a large percentage of the reasons the proliferation of mass shootings in public schools. Indeed, it is their ungodly love of power/money that causes them to blindly refuse to fix the problem simply by demanding sensible gun control legislation.

Do Americans need to be reminded that: "Lo, children are an heritage of the Lord: and the fruit of the womb is his reward"? (Psalm 127:3). America's children are in harm's way daily because of political-economic corruption. Public school violence is a national spiritual-moral crisis. The students of Marjory Stoneman Douglas High School in Parkland, Florida, pricked the national conscience of America with their dogged determination to confront the issue of gun violence head-on. Regrettably, children are fighting a spiritual-political battle that adults have the political power (vote) to resolve for them to change the situational equation. Unfortunately, without any positive political and legislative consideration from the majority Political Party (RNC), just changing guns laws will not cure the problem. Shame! Shame! Shame!

Just maybe, Americans need to remind themselves of the sins of the past and the resulting socio-economic consequences. More importantly, we need to get busy resolving the critical issues of the twenty-first century as it relates to public school education and the psychological harm being heaped upon the heads of our children.

After all, education is the key to the American Dream. Hence, the issue of public school safety must be resolved now, not later. This issue alone is socio-psychologically destroying the mental psyche of the nation's children to feel safe and secure in public school environments. Public schools should not be combat zones. Therefore, Christian Right Evangelicals, "Put up again thy sword into his place: for all they that take the sword shall perish with the sword" (Matthew 26:52).

Guns do not solve the problem of evil (gun-violence) in public school environments. Just maybe, the Founders of America's democratic Constitutional system of governance, and their desire to create a mass universal public school system so that every individual learn to read; especially learn to read the Bible was the correct approach. The question is: Where did America go wrong in the practical spiritual implementation of educational developmental processes, as well as the implementation of public school educational systems? "Blessed is he that readeth, and they that hear the words of this prophecy, and keep those things which are written therein: for the time is at hand" (Revelation 1:3).

Spiritual awareness, ethical consciousness, and moral order (conduct) must always have a role in public school education. When individuals take God (truth) out of any socio-economic-political institution, one can expect disastrous consequences and doom-day failure. The long and the short of it is, we must all take heed because thus saith the Lord: "Come now, and let us reason together, saith the Lord: though your sins be as scarlet, they shall be as white as snow; though they be red like crimson; they shall be as wool. If ye be willing and obedient, ye shall eat the good of the land" (Isaiah 1:18-19).

- Since everyone agrees that children are our future, let's not just talk about it (their future), let's be about it. Thus, America, here are some public safety and security measures that we need to diligently institute in public school environments for the public safety and well-being of students:

- The passage of strict gun-control laws, especially those that relate to military-style weaponry in conjunction with the closing of gun-show loop-holes.

- The strengthening of mental health background check laws for the purchase of guns.

- Public school physical facilities must be made safer and more secure.

- Public school districts should institute professional sensitivity training programs for administrators and teachers to identify emotionally-mentally-challenged-troubled students: A social services system. The spiritual-moral breakdown of family life in American society has fueled the emotional-mental instability of children. Institute professional processes for students to anonymously report mentally-challenged students.

- All school districts should institute public relations programs with local law enforcement officials to encourage students to: "if you see something or hear something, say something": Police school community relations program.
- Unfortunately, public school districts might have to resort to security-check-point systems.

The American Dream is a reality for most, but, unfortunately for some whites it is a nightmare; simply because of personal and family-related experiences, attitudes, and moral values. These circumstances exist primarily because of institutional racism (White Privilege) and personal/moral attitudes and values. A prime example was the school shooting at Columbine. America's public school children must learn how to creatively and non-violently resolve social conflict through positive socialization. This must be done by embracing truth, not lies. Individuals should never make telling lies a profession. For example: the foundation of racism is based upon a lie. Individuals who cannot accept that equal is equal have no God-conscience.

Parents should never make racially derogatory statements about other races, ethnicities, or cultures in family settings. All parents should always remember that your children are not only your spiritual heritage, but they are an extension of your physical and social being. Finally, parents, "I beseech you therefore, brethren, by the mercies of God, that ye present your bodies a living sacrifice, holy acceptable unto God, which is your reasonable service. And be not conformed to this world: but be ye transformed by the renewing of your mind, that ye may prove what is that, good and acceptable, and perfect, will of God" (Romans 12:1-2).

America, the will of God is simply: "Love God and love each other." Amen!

What Happened To Black Society?

Prior to the passage of the 1964 Civil Rights Act and the 1965 Voting Rights Act, the systematized, legalized dehumanization of Blacks by law demanded a collectivistic approach to life as it related to economic development, educational development, and socio-religious development. Blacks were forced into functioning as a nation within a nation; therefore, they had no choice but to share resources on a higher level of spirituality and morality. The black church became "black society" that epitomizes the black community. Of course, it is better to live together as Americans rather than as "divided, we fall." By the way, we did declare, constitutionally, that "We Are One Nation Under God." Unfortunately, the greed for money and power, coupled with racial-tribalism keeps us divided from each other as Americans. Even U.S. currency is inscribed with these sacred words: "In God We Trust."

What does all of this mean? It means that for too many Americans it is only symbolism, not spiritual reality; thus, making money is equivalent to God. Seemingly, the majority of Americans have lost their way in terms of achieving and maintaining a democratic-godly society. The ungodly desire for White Privilege has polluted White thought processes to the degree that minorities are not permitted the opportunity to demonstrate how to live one with another in peace according to the Two Great Commandments of Jesus. Additionally, the election of Donald J. Trump to the Office of President has become a frightening moral-leadership reminder of that socio-spiritual fact of American life. Life in America with Donald J. Trump as President is, indeed, chaos to the nth degree.

The "White Only" signs were visible pictorial reminders that the destiny of Blacks was inextricably tied together and you had better not forget it, "PhD or No D." Unfortunately, some Blacks accepted the racial mandates of that ERA (racial dehumanization) and allowed themselves to be mummified by fear and embraced an individualistic approach to life. The election of President Donald J. Trump is a stark twenty-first century wake-up call. Black people must stay vigilant and never take an inch backwards, because The Donald J. Trumps of America, in conjunction with Christian Right Evangelicals, and the greedy money-changers of America are working toward the demise of minorities. Blacks must change their socio-economic paradigm, or else they will perish. Hence, the inability of Blacks to maintain a focused sense of morality from one generation to the next has had profound socio-spiritual-disintegration consequences on both families as well as churches. Thus, it is a spiritually and morally imperative that Blacks love and serve each other as well as others (fellowman), because it is God's will and command!

Sinfully, and without a doubt, some "white folks" are always going to be "white folks" looking for an excuse to explain away their personal failures. Thus, America to them was, as Judge Roy Moore declared, "America was great when slavery existed". Of course, most God-fearing Americans believe that slavery was America's original sin, not its greatness. Shame! Shame! Shame! Even though the law has changed, some individuals cannot and will not obey the law, because they do not know the Spiritual Law-giver: GOD. The law concerning work was given when the entrance to the Garden of Eden was sealed by God to all humankind, and life was no longer a free gift. Men must work by the sweat of their brow. God's universal commandment concerning work is recorded in Genesis 4:17-19: Every man must work by the sweat of his own brow because "cursed is the ground for thy sake."

The Law is the law and justice is spiritual. Thus, the basis for Justice is just Laws. For example: Jesus was asked by the religious hypocrites of His era should they pay taxes to Caesar. Jesus answered: "Whose image and superscription hath it? Why tempt me? . . . Render therefore unto Caesar the things which be Caesar's and unto God the things which be God's" (Luke 20:23, 25). Life is not about extremes. Individuals do not have control over either the circumstances of their birth or death. But, individuals do have free-will and the devil is your enemy. In the case of suicide, an individual has broken faith with himself or herself; therefore, if an individual is willing to commit suicide, he/she has made a suicide pact with the devil. Why kill yourself? Just have patience and wait because death is inevitable. Everything changes. Nothing remains the same. Just keep on living.

God spiritually commanded that men love and protect their wives as well as provide spiritual-moral leadership and material substance for family units. Women should teach, by example, love in the context of family interaction. This is why families should spiritually and prayerfully choose church houses for family worship with the upmost spiritual consideration, because broken homes engender broken churches and vice-versa. Let's not forget, society begins and ends in the family unit(s).

The lack of quality educational environments in the black

community has become a monumental spiritual-moral impediment to civility. Since the desegregation of public education in 1954, America has steadily been marching toward a spiritual-moral mental as well as an educational bankruptcy of minds. The decline in public educational environments is associated with a number of factors: home environments, neighborhood environments, administrative management, and teacher quality.

Racist legal structures and white public attitudinal disdain as displayed by "White Only" signs spiritually forced Blacks into living from the inside to the outside. The removal of physical legal structures and public signs of dehumanization gave some Blacks a false sense of "Free at last, thank God almighty, I'm free at last." Of course, freedom is a spiritual internal state of being and not physical mobility. Nelson Mandala was free even while in a South African prison. Martin L. King, Jr. was free even while in the Birmingham Jail with his "Letter From the Birmingham Jail" as the spiritual testament thereto. Kunta Kinte was free, even after losing a foot, in running from White oppression in his mind. Jesus was free even though nailed (crucified) on a cross on Calvary's Hill, dying for the sins of a spiritually sin-sick world. Now, too many Blacks are dealing with freedom as external, that is, the physical right to go anywhere at any time as well as the ability to acquire things. Material things do not make individuals happy or free. And, if they did, everyone would be happy and peace on earth would exist. Greed and tribalism is a dangerous combination; therefore, "Take heed, and beware of covetousness: for a man's life consisteth not in the abundance of the things which he possesseth" (Luke 12:15). Selah!

The Power of Divine Love

"For God so loved the world, that he gave his only begotten Son, that whosoever believeth in him should not perish, but have everlasting life" (John 3:16). This is why the power of divine love transcends all man-made social distinctions of race/ethnicity, social class distinctions, and economic statuses. The election of Barack Obama and his world class family residing in The White House was an expression of God's divine love for America as well as the world. The selection of Pope Francis as the spiritual leader of Catholicism which we know as The Catholic Church was another divine act of God. And, the marriage of Prince Harry to an American interracial woman, Meghan, was another divine act of God's love for this sin-sick world. What a loving God we serve! Of course, it is only because of God's divine love that even President Donald J. Trump can make a difference in a sin-sick world.

Born-again, blood-bought Christians (Christ-like) need to "Come boldly unto the throne of grace, that we may obtain mercy, and find grace to help in time of need" (Hebrews 4:16). This is why we as Christians should offer this prayer to God on behalf of the leadership of Donald J. Trump, the forty-fifth President of these United States of America: "He hath shewed thee, O man, what is good: and what doth the Lord require of thee, but to do justly, and to love mercy, and to walk humbly with thy God" (Micah 6:8).

America, as long as we have pastoral leaders such as Bishop Michael Curry of the Episcopal Church, who gave the sermon at the wedding of Prince Harry and Meghan as well as pastors such as Dr. Robert Childress, Pastor Walter August, Pastor Terry Anderson, Pastor Raymond Farley, Pastor Reginald DeVaughn, Pastor Ralph West, Dr. Charles Stanley, Bishop L.J. Woodward, Jr., Pastor I. V. Hilliard, Dr. Ed. Young, Pastor Gusta Booker, Pastor Max Miller, Pastor Roland Robinson and Pastor John Morgan—all individuals who rightfully divide God's spiritual truth concerning love, peace, and joy, we will have individuals living in peace and spiritual harmony under the sovereignty of God. We have great men and women of God who do not look back at sin, nor ask the question, Lord will you accept ten (10)? Of course, we do have thousands, and I can't name them all or attempt to do so!

The spiritual jury is still out on Pastor Kirbyjon Caldwell; therefore, we humbly beseech and pray for Your divine presence in the life of

President Trump, that he might learn to love You with all of his heart, soul, mind, and strength, and love and serve others in Jesus' name, and not himself nor his family and friends because "Hatred stirreth up strifes: but love covereth all sins" (Proverbs 10:12).

In 2008, God through His divine love and mercy allowed America to begin a spiritual healing process to institutionally redeem itself from its original sin: Slavery and Institutional Racism. The election of President Barack Obama and the quality conduct of their family life in The White House absolutely demonstrated that Americans can love and serve one another in peace. Yes, we can! The Republican Party, in conjunction with certain Democratic operatives, sought with all of their power and might to limit President Obama's accomplishments. But we all know, "What shall we say to these things? If God be for us, who can be against us?" (Romans 8:31).

In 2013, The College of Cardinals realized that Jorge Mario Bergoglio, Pope Francis, was the "best of the best" to lead Catholicism in this era of spiritual uncertainty to restore wandering believers. In fact, Pope Francis has all of the spiritual attributes required for moral leadership in the twenty-first century. "Let him know, that he which converteth the sinner from the error of his way shall save a soul from death, and shall hide a multitude of sins" (James 5:20).

"Whoso findeth a wife findeth a good thing, and obtaineth favor of the Lord" (Proverb 18:22). The marriage of Prince Harry and Meghan spiritually symbolized unity of heart, soul, and mind, and brought to mind these scriptural words of inspiration: "Can two walk together, except they be agreed?" (Amos 3:3). All three of these major historical events were expressions of God's unwavering love for us regardless of race/ethnicity, religion, or socio-economic statuses. Thus, if you did not understand in your heart and mind to trust Jesus, you need a faith check "For when we were yet without strength, in due time Christ died for the ungodly. For scarcely for a righteous man will one die: yet peradventure for a good man some would even dare to die. But God commendeth his love toward us, in that, while we were yet sinners, Christ died for us" (Romans 5:6-8).

Moreover, God wants all of us to know "How shall we escape, if we neglect so great salvation; which at the first began to be spoken by the Lord..." (Hebrews 2:3). Take heed, Christian Right Evangelicals, The Republican Party, and President Trump: "The fear of the Lord is to hate evil: pride, and arrogancy, and the evil way, and the froward mouth, do I hate" (Proverbs 8:13). Bishop Michael Curry in his sermon at the Royal wedding of Prince Harry and Meghan reminded the world that the power and love of God covers a multitude of sins.

In the three historic events referenced in this editorial, God in the universal language of love was seeking to redeem universal humanity and at the same time, telling all humanity: "GET OVER IT." God is God Almighty and His love covers the sins of racism, sexism, and classism as well as any other arbitrary human "ISM." Hence, the characteristics of love are like fire shut up in your bones, running in your feet, clapping in your hands, placing joy in your heart and:

"Though I speak with the tongues of men and of angels, and have not charity, I am become as sounding brass, or a tinkling cymbal.

And though I have the gift of prophecy, and understand all mysteries, and all knowledge; and though I have all faith, so that I could remove mountains, and have not charity, I am nothing.

And though I bestow all of my goods to feed the poor, and though I give my body to be burned, and have not charity, it profiteth me nothing.

Charity suffereth long, and is kind: charity envieth not; charity vaunteth not itself, is not puffed up,

Doth not behave itself unseemly, seeketh not her own, is not easily provoked, thinketh no evil;

Rejoiceth not in iniquity, but rejoiceth in the truth;

Beareth all things, believeth all things, hopeth all things, endureth all things.

Charity never faileth: but whether there be prophecies, they shall fail; whether there be tongues, they shall cease; whether there be knowledge, it shall vanish away.

For we know in part, and we prophesy in part.

But when that which is perfect is come, then that which is in part shall be done away.

When I was a child, I spake as a child, I understood as a child, I thought as a child: but when I became a man, I put away childish things.

For now we see through a glass, darkly; but then face to face: now I know in part; but then shall I know even as also I am known.

And now abideth faith, hope, charity, these three; but the greatest of these is charity."

—1 Corinthians 13:1-13

Charity is godly love. Selah!

National Football League (NFL): National Faith League

Football is America's favorite past-time, and, at the same time, it provides some of the most integrated social activities in American society. On the other hand, 11:00 AM on Sunday morning is the most segregated hour in American society as well as a socio-philosophical oxymoron. Just think about it. The reality is, Americans can "play" together, but, for some ungodly socio-religious-psychological reason(s), and they cannot worship God in spirit and truth together. America's governing documents are grounded in spiritual concepts, and "God is a Spirit: and they that worship him must worship him in spirit and in truth" (John 4:24).

The Bible declares that there is a right time and place for

everything: "To everything there is a season, and a time to every purpose under heaven: A time to rend, and a time to sew; a time to keep silence, and a time to speak" (Ecclesiastes 3:1, 7). There is a time for kneeling against social injustice, and there is a time for standing up against injustices (unrighteousness) and moving forward righteously in changing institutional structures of injustice.

The National Football League has an important role it can play in helping to change societal institutional structures of social injustice. Recently, some NFL players began kneeling during the playing of the National Anthem in order to not "become bitter, but to become better" by calling attention to the issue of police brutality and misconduct. The NFL must morally play an important socio-psychological role in helping its players (or gladiators), especially black players, learn how to leave aggression on the football field, and to realize they do not have to be the spiritual inspiration for resolving societal ills that they did not create.

Therefore, in every franchise city, as part of its expected community engagement-conscience-building activities, the NFL should provide resources and suggestions to police departments for minority cultural group-sensitivity training. This would be an important beginning point for societal healing, if everyone understood that charity begins at home and then spreads elsewhere (like to nonfranchise cities). Moreover, the NFL should establish a blue-ribbon commission and a governmental-lobbying process for both local and state entities to deal with the issue of police-community relations. Although, as Americans, we all have the same battles, football players should not have to fight Civil Rights battles against societal injustices; they have their own personal as well as professional battles.

For example: after a difficult practice session and a hard fought game, some players have emotional difficulties (adrenalin highs) in socially interacting with others. These types of football personalities need some creative down time and counseling before interacting with others; especially family members. Hence, NFL management must become sensitive to these types of player personalities on a team. In the midst of the most highly-charged profile issue of the twenty-first century, President Trump injected partisan politics and personal animosity into the equation. He challenged NFL owners in a misguided and ungodly manner by suggesting that owners violate the Civil Rights of players as a way to deflect attention from his poor approval ratings.

NFL owners are not plantation masters with high-paid slaves, and, therefore, cannot arbitrarily violate Civil Rights Laws to impose their will. The First Amendment to the Constitution gives citizens the right to protest peacefully. We all know that President Trump's comments were simply a deflection tactic to cover-up his ineptness as a Presidential leader. What the President suggested could ultimately bankrupt the NFL, and we all know that President Trump understands bankruptcy since he has filed four times. The NFL solution to the police-community problem must start with NFL players, the NFL commissioner, ownership management, player union representatives, mayors, chiefs-of-police departments, and police union representatives buying into a suitable process with great sensitivity on all sides.

Once again, on Sundays the NFL has become a highly integrated-multicultural social-economic enterprise at every level: fan participation, players, and referees. At the same time, Christian Right Evangelical churches are highly segregated institutions. Maybe Christian Right Evangelical churches should institute an NFL-type policy that is a National Faith League oriented toward spiritual unity/inclusion among Americans especially Christians. In the twenty-first century, Christian church unity is sorely needed because, seemingly, Christian Right Evangelical pastors are apparently preaching and teaching a different gospel than the Gospel that is taught in Bible-based Christian churches. Sometimes perception is greater than the truth; but, in the final analysis the truth is the TRUTH. God has the last word. God is love and the truth has its origin with God, and a lie is the devil. All Americans have a mind to think, a heart to love, and a spiritual conscience to have a relationship with God in the remission of their sins. Most importantly, we must realize that Jesus, the Righteous One, is our Intercessor to God.

President Trump, eighty-one percent (81%) of Christian Right Evangelicals who voted, voted for you in the 2016 Presidential election. Without a doubt, National Faith Leaders (NFL) is central to the spiritual health and well-being of American society, because without a spiritual understanding of God and self, a nation-state perishes. The National Football League is highly integrated and reflects the multicultural nature of American society. Mr. President, you have an opportunity to speak truth to evil, and challenge Christian Right Evangelical Church leaders knowing full well that the churches they pastor are highly segregated. Furthermore, it is time for Christian Right Church goers to stop standing up tall in false pride, and, instead, get down on their knees with humility, for the truth and righteousness of God. Remember honor comes through humility.

This will definitely negate the double standard in Christian Right Evangelical church houses of worship, and, just maybe, this might help drain the "Swamp" in Washington as well as State Houses of governmental representation. We all need to help America become the city on a hill for the entire world to see and admire. Executive orders cannot eliminate racism, nor can laws change the hearts of individuals. But, national faith leaders, can begin to teach the truth of God that equal is equal, not equal is more or less equal. God hates racism and we should never forget that spiritual fact.

NFL commissioner and team owners, after the kneeling protest, we will still be divided as a nation. So, what comes next? Obviously, socio-spiritual-programmatic efforts must be creatively and professionally conceived and implemented to heal the racial divide. Selah!

The NFL: Property Rights Versus Human Rights?

"He hath shewed thee, O man (POTUS 45), what is good; and what doth the Lord require of thee, but to do justly, and to love mercy, and to walk humbly with thy God." (Micah 6:8). America, why can't we take heed and spiritually-morally understand, especially Christian Right Evangelicals and National Football League Owners (NFL), that we should do justly, love mercy, and spiritually-morally walk humbly with God because "The Lord's voice crieth unto the city (America), and the man (individuals) of wisdom shall see thy name: hear ye the rod (truth), and who hath appointed it" (Micah 6:9).

"Are there yet the treasures of wickedness in the house of the wicked, and the scant measure that is abominable?" (Micah 6:10). Christian Right Evangelicals, what is your answer to God's question in (Micah 6:10)? Be careful in answering this question because in your answer there is spiritual condemnation. But, it is through spiritual condemnation that we all receive salvation. Likewise, there are some NFL owners who were million-dollar contributors to the Trump Campaign effort, thereby helping to fuel national confusion in America's political processes. Now, even in America's national past-time, a spiritual-moral debate has been ignited over kneeling for social justice. Are NFL Football Franchise Organizations slave plantations: Property Rights versus Human Rights? According to the public declarations of two owners of Texas franchises, they are. And, of course, the silence of other NFL owners is consent to the proposition that all men are not created equal in dignity contrary to the Preamble to the U.S. Constitution!

By the way, Christian Right Evangelicals, ornate church houses do not please God. God does not dwell in temples made by hands. "For we know that if our earthly house of this tabernacle were dissolved, we have a building of God, an house not made with hands, eternal in the heavens" (2 Corinthians 5:1). God wants His children to be living sacrifices of fairness, just doing, and righteous living. Hence, it is impossible to consistently follow God without His transforming love in the heart of your mind.

It is, indeed, unfortunate that some NFL owners are fostering spiritual-moral confusion in America's greatest past-time (NFL

Football) by raising the question of property rights versus human rights. Of course, this set of circumstances exists because Christian Right Evangelical Pastoral Leaders refuse to preach the truth of God because of monetary gain. Why, Why, Why, O Lord, when God supplies every need. America, it is as difficult for some rich men to go to Heaven as it is for a camel to go through the eye of a needle. Hear America: "For the rich men (Some NFL Owners) thereof are full of violence, and the inhabitants thereof have spoken lies, and their tongue is deceitful in their mouth" (Micah 6:12). After all, some rich men like Trump administration officials are willing to take America to the brink of war or even to war by telling chronic-habitual lies. Trump administration officials are chronic habitual liars. True spiritual justice shall prevail because true justice does not come through the barrel of guns. "Then said Jesus unto him, Put up again thy sword into his place: for all they that take the sword shall perish with the sword" (Matthew 26:52). Currently, America has a civilian governmental system controlled by a militaristic mentality in civilian attire, especially in the Trump White House.

The election of Donald J. Trump as the forty-fifth President of the United States appears to have had assistance from an ungodly Russian thumb on the scales of democracy. Because of Russian interference in our democratic processes, America is now on spiritual trial before the nation-states of the world while almighty

God is the Righteous Judge. Sadly, some NFL owners, because of personal unprofessional statements, have placed themselves on public trial as well.

There is a big difference between partisan politics and public policy. Partisan politics are about particularistic privileges for the few. Public policy is about universal common good for all. Discrimination and the dehumanization of black Americans was historic institutionalized public policy/law; hence, the Texan franchise owner's statement "We can't have the prisoners in charge of the prison" is not just a proverbial slip of a rich man's tongue, but a spiritual mind-set. The "Eyes of Texas" might be on these two owners (Jones and McNair), but surely the spiritual eye of God is on both of these powerful rich men.

"Shall I count them pure with the wicked balances, and with the bag of deceitful weights?" (Micah 6:1). The rich and powerful are never satisfied because the Bible says so. "Thou shalt eat, but not be satisfied; and thy casting down shall be in the midst of thee; and thou shalt take hold, but shall not deliver; and that which thou deliverest will I give up to the sword" (Micah 6:14). Ungodly individuals are never satisfied; therefore, they must invariably and consistently involve themselves in afflicting evil on others. When your faith is in your currency (money), not in the spiritual statement written on the currency, "In God We Trust," you are worshipping an idol god. "For the love of money is the root of all evil: which while some coveted after, they have erred from the faith, and pierced themselves through with many sorrows" (1 Timothy 6:10). Just because some spiritually-confused individuals control the circulation of money, they think they are God. If the truth be told, they are not even small gods with a small "g". But, they just might be a god spelled backwards.

Moreover, black Americans know full well the socio-economic distance they have come, realizing at the same time that egalitarian economic justice still does not exist; therefore, every Christian believer knows that we are spiritually light years away from "Heaven on earth" (The Lord's Prayer).

Houstonians and all sports franchise owners, as we celebrate our first of many to come World Series victories, lest we forget, it was primarily the visionary leadership of Houston's first black mayor, Lee P. Brown, who gave us three world-class state-of-the-art sports facilities. Moreover, Texan franchise owner, Robert McNair, when thinking of your economic prison system investment which, in turn, has doubled over the years, think of the leadership mentality of Mayor Lee P. Brown. Thank God!

March Madness!

"March Madness" in 2017, is not about college basketball but the Presidential leadership mentality in The White House that has produced an April fool's Joke. Without a doubt, this April, American society experienced a monumental crisis of Presidential leadership governance unlike any other in its history. Moreover, America has an intellectual integrity, a moral character, and a crisis of conscience Presidential leadership problem, not just a political governance problem. Getting elected does not mean that you are worthy of electability. It may simply mean that you were able to hood-wink the right-wrong-thinking voters in the right Electoral College States. My fellow Americans, "I beseech you therefore, brethren, by the mercies of God, that ye present your bodies a living sacrifice, holy acceptable unto God, which is your reasonable service. And be not conformed to this world: but be ye transformed by the renewing of your mind, that ye may prove what is that good, and acceptable, and perfect, will of God" (Romans 1:1-2). America, it is not too late through legal channels/impeachment to throw the ungodly bums out of the White House; especially before they turn America over to Putin and a Russian State, without firing a shot, but by destroying our democratic institutions in the process.

America, our institutional structures cannot withstand perpetual Presidential and institutional lying. Americans must be told the truth and nothing but the truth especially from the Oval Office because "Let every soul be subject unto the higher powers. For there is no power but of God: the powers that be are ordained of God. Whosoever therefore resisteth the power, resisteth the ordinance of God: and they that resist shall receive to themselves damnation" (Romans 13:1-2). A lie cannot stand. A lie can only deflect momentarily until it is challenged, again and again. Truth will prevail. America, permit God to "Sanctify them through thy truth: thy word is truth" (John 17:17). Because: "Ye shall know the truth, and the truth shall make you free" (John 8:32). Any casual spiritual observer who understands socio-economic facts, and who watched the repeal and replace Obamacare circus should by now clearly understand that most white males can only be in agreement when dealing with clearly defined majority-minority situations. Get over it! America, let's build an inclusive democratic society because we must teach our children as well as future generations how to forgive. Minorities, especially black Americans, have forgiven the past. The past belongs to the devil.

Some Americans, seemingly, just can't get over it. Without a doubt, what is currently transpiring in American society is all about White Privilege. Of course, some Americans have an insatiable appetite for power and money, which in turn, drives them to sell-out America for thirty-pieces of silver (foreign or domestic) which is a Biblical financial term for unethical behavior. Of course, lying and ethnic conflicts are not making America great again, but making America the ugly American in the spiritual eye-sight of the world community. Moreover, America's intellectual integrity and spiritual-moral character foundation is being eroded (destroyed) for the sake of White Privilege for a few Whites. Simply put: greed and power do not permit room at the top for all Whites because absolute power corrupts absolutely.

As adults, we must teach and remind each other that our children are a gift from God, that the future belongs to God, that our children are our future in God for building the Kingdom of God on earth as it is in heaven, that to forgive is divine, and that they should always be peacemakers. "Lo, children are an heritage of the Lord: and the fruit of the womb is his reward" (Psalm 127:3). More importantly, we must teach our children how to become peace-makers and not war-mongers. Hence, "Blessed are the peacemakers: for they shall be called the children of God. Blessed are the pure in heart for they shall see God. Blessed are the merciful for they shall obtain mercy. Blessed are they which do hunger and thirst after righteousness: for they shall be filled" (Matthew 5:6-9).

Forewarned is foretold. The ungodly governmental lying must stop; especially the Presidential lying, because what is at stake is the future of American society as we know it. Great nations rise and fall simply because of an immoral leader's desire to become the master of the world. Jesus is Lord and Master. "For with the heart man believeth unto righteousness; and with the mouth confession is made unto salvation" (Romans 10:10). Since January 20th, 2017, from his own mouth the forty-fifth President" has dishonored himself as well as all Americans by consistently lying and having other governmental officials lie for him. For after all, from the heart of his own mind he has told us precisely how he feels about minorities, women, certain religions, and individuals with political opinions different from his own.

Jesus is Lord and Master because of this Scriptural verse penned by the Gospel writer Paul: "For I say, through the grace given unto me, to every man that is among you, not to think of himself more highly than he ought to think; but to think soberly, according as God hath dealt to every man the measure of faith" (Romans 12:3). Therefore, Christian America, "Let every soul be subject unto the high powers.

For there is no power but of God" (Romans 13:1). Every American, let's boldly celebrate the resurrection of our Lord and Savior, Jesus Christ the Righteous One. Selah!

Why We Kneel

God is good all the time and His mercy endures forever. Right and wrong are not relative. Right is right and wrong is wrong. The law is based upon truth and facts. Hence, equal is equal, not more or less equal. More importantly, this is precisely why Lady Justice is blind. The Holy Spirit frees us from sin. "There is therefore now no condemnation to them which are in Christ Jesus, who walk not after the flesh, but after the Spirit. For the law of the spirit of life in Christ Jesus hath made me free from the law of sin and death. For what the law could not do, in that it was weak through the flesh, God sending his own Son in the likeness of sinful flesh, and for sin, condemned sin in the flesh: that the righteousness of the law might be fulfilled in us, who walk not after the flesh, but after the Spirit" (Romans 8:1-4).

Why is President Trump condemning the National Football League? Is it because he was not given the opportunity to acquire a franchise? Without a doubt, if he owned a NFL franchise, American taxpayers would not have to see his income taxes to know, that he is truly a billionaire! Christian Right Evangelicals please inform President Trump that "God judgeth the righteous, and God is angry with the wicked every day" (Psalm 7:11). America, please do not gamble with this Biblical verse because ". . . as it is appointed unto men once to die, but after this the judgment" (Hebrews 9:27).

Congressman Shelia Jackson-Lee, a woman of God, knelt on the House of Representative floor in honor of God, country, and justice for all—especially for Puerto Rico. Representative Shelia Jackson-Lee took to the House floor Monday night to kneel in solidarity with NFL players who chose to defy President Trump and protest police brutality. Congresswoman Jackson-Lee said, "You cannot deny that President Trump calling NFL players who kneel a "son of a bitch" is racism. There is no regulation that says these young men cannot stand against the dishonoring of their mothers by you calling for the firing of a "son-of-a-bitch". That is racism. You cannot deny it, you cannot run from it, and I kneel in honor of them. I kneel in front of the flag and on this floor. I kneel in honor of the First Amendment. I kneel because the flag is a symbol for freedom. I kneel because I'm going to stand against racism. I kneel because I will stand with those young men and I will stand with our soldiers. And I'll stand with America, because I kneel. The only reason he is doing this is that someone had the lack of judgment to provoke the situation and call their mothers a name. I refuse to accept that as a standard of leadership for the highest office in the world. Even if you never understand it, sir, if you think you're playing to your base, we will continue to stand in the gap, and racism is going to be under our feet. You know where else it is going to be? Under our knees!"

There are some white Americans who embrace devilish notions of ungodly White Privilege simply because their desire is to not share the American Dream with minority Americans, especially black Americans. Living from the outside (external-materialism) to the inside (internal-spirituality) will utterly confuse an individual about who he is, and who he is ultimately accountable to. Hence, spiritual-minded individuals act like children of God, not like children of Cain.

There is a spiritual message in just kneeling. Down through the ages great men have always knelt and prostrated themselves before God Almighty, the maker of all things. Christian Right Evangelicals, why not try kneeling before Almighty God—unless your sense of false-pride has polluted your mind (brain) and heart (spiritual-conscience) and your desire to be godlike. After all, a Christian knows to "Be careful for nothing; but in everything by prayer and supplication with thanksgiving let your requests be made known unto God. And the peace of God, which passeth all understanding, shall keep your hearts and minds through Christ Jesus" (Philippians

4:6-7). There is more joy in giving than taking or receiving.

There is a right, and there is a wrong; they are not the same in either God's law or man's law. God gave us the Ten Commandments as well as Scriptures of inspiration to live by. On top of that, God gave us free-will (human-right choices). If an individual chooses to not live by God's laws, he/she can die and go to hell. Of course, "There is a way which seemeth right unto a man, but the end thereof are the ways of death" (Proverbs 14:12). There is a hell. The Bible says so. In 1776, the Founders gave us a Preamble to the U.S. Constitution and Articles of the Constitution stating the bases for your human rights as an American. The First Article of the U.S. Constitution is the right to peacefully protest. That's the law, so either obey the law or change the law. We are a nation of laws (Civil and Criminal), everyone must obey the law, and no one is above the law, not even the President. Most white owners of NFL teams, if not all, gave President Trump one-million dollars. Black NFL Players did not utter a word even though they understood the sexist, racist, and religious bigotry of Donald J. Trump.

In high dollar bidding competitions, Fox Sports Network was awarded the NFL contract to air NFL games. By any reasonable journalistic standard, Fox News Network is not fair and balanced in reporting truth based upon facts. Without a doubt, Fox News is the epitome of alternative facts. Once again, black NFL players did not utter a mumbling word. It appears as though President Trump for socio-economic-political reasons (EGO: Edge God Out) is seeking to destroy the economic foundation of the NFL. Let's hope that it is not out of resentment, because at one time Trump sought an opportunity to own the Buffalo Bills Franchise, but was rejected (turned-down). Thank God!

Black Americans have been on their knees seeking righteous judgment for almost four hundred years in American society. But-God! Prayer changes things from the spiritual inside to the moral and spiritual outside, and the law is made weak through the flesh. Morality cannot be legislated! America, beware! Christian Right Evangelicals in collaboration with President Donald J. Trump are "Professing themselves to be wise, they became fools, and changed the glory of the uncorruptible God into an image made like to corruptible man" (Romans 1:22-23).

Congresswoman Shelia Jackson-Lee, faith in God and know that the race is not given to the swift, or the battle to the strong. No individual knows his time (when the death angel shall call your name). Moreover, continue to kneel, and, likewise, Americans of spiritual-moral conscience will kneel with you. Therefore, "How shall we escape, if we neglect so great salvation" (Hebrews 2:3).

America, know full well that black Americans kneel to Almighty God to become better, not bitter. Selah!

The Extermination of Rocket-Man

President Trump is by far the most unpopular President in the stoic history of American society. Of course, his Christian Right Evangelical supporters and the Republican Party are equally as unpopular, because of their love of power and money. For it has been declared "Therefore we are always confident, knowing that, whilst we are at home in the body, we are absent from the Lord: (for we walk by faith, not by sight :) we are confident, I say, and willing rather to be absent from the body, and to be present with the Lord. Wherefore we labor, that, whether present or absent, we may be accepted of him. For we must all appear before the judgment seat of Christ; that everyone may receive the things done in his body, according to that he hath done, whether it be good or bad" (2 Corinthians 5:6-10). President Obama was unpopular with some Americans simply because he was black. At the same time, he was among America's most popular Presidents internationally primarily because of his intellect and statesman-like qualities. President Obama possessed great professionalism, dignity, and grace. This is why he was called "No Drama, Obama."

One of the many reasons Christian Right Evangelical voters voted eighty-one percent (81%) for President Trump was their desire to wipe-the-slate-clean of every vestige of a historic Presidency. Clearly, they still have a problem with the color of a man's skin, and they spiritually incubated this in their hearts and minds. But, we all know "God judgeth the righteous, and God is angry with the wicked every day" (Psalm 7:11). Christian Right Evangelicals hated the man because of the color of his skin, not the content of his character. Unfortunately, they still do. But God hates sin and so should Christian Right Evangelicals. If weapons of war could solve nation-state-problems then given the mighty arsenals of war that Russia and the United States have they should have no problems. Thank God they cannot! For, after all, weapons of war only maim, destroy, kill, and cause tremendous human suffering. War is not the answer! God is the answer because "The earth is the Lord's, and the fullness thereof; the world, and they that dwell therein" (Psalm 24:1).

In relationship to the North Korean nuclear problem and President Trump's nomenclature for the Supreme Leader of North Korea (Rocket-Man), President Trump has said, "You Will See." I put forth a theoretical question: Has President Trump instructed U.S. Military Officials to orchestrate an illegal process of assassination of North Korea's Supreme Leader Kim Jong-Un? Just maybe, this is not a plausible moral-governing-theory for a democratic nation-state. Democratic nation-states do not order the assassinations of heads of foreign governments. President Obama's ordering of the "taking-out" of Osama Bin Laden, an international terrorist killer, who bragged about killing over 3,000 Americans at one time (9/11) is not moral equivalency. Is this the reason the President's answer to the National Press Core's question concerning North Korea is always: "You Will See"? Moreover, is this the reason he has said to Secretary of State Tillerson: "You Are Wasting Your Time"? President Trump obviously knows that the "Die Is Cast." Being envious of the abilities and accomplishments of a black man is worse than a jealous husband who cannot go to work, because he is always policing his wife's behavior.

De-certifying the Iran Nuclear Agreement is another glaring politically unwise example of President Trump's political goals as well as his malnutrition-of-the-brain-oriented obsession with the accomplishments of the Obama Administration. Trump and his Christian Right Evangelical supporters have with erasing the history of a black man as President since day one, (the birther movement). Secretary of State Tillerson reportedly called President Trump the

Commander-in-Chief a moron. When asked did he call President Trump a moron, he did not vehemently refute the allegation. What is it that Secretary Tillerson knows that the American people should be made aware of?

Moreover, Senator Corker of Tennessee, Chairman of the Foreign Relations Committee, stated publicly that President Trump is leading the country into World War III. Again I ask, what is it that Senator Corker knows that the American people should be aware of? Unfortunately, too many Americans, especially Republican Officials and Christian Right Evangelicals are going along to get along without realizing you cannot get along with someone the Secretary of State has publicly called a moron. Without a doubt, if Americans see the mushroom cloud, it's too late. Wake up Republicans: silence is consent! Therefore, stand up and speak out now before it is too late.

These statements by Republican Officials are cause for great concern for our sons and daughters who are our future as a nation-state. President Johnson called America's future "The Great Society." God has blessed America and is still blessing America in spite of withholding His righteous judgment. Christian Right Evangelicals of the Trump-God persuasion, stop worshipping a secularized man, and start worshipping God, "For there is one God, and one mediator between God and men, the man Christ Jesus" (1 Timothy 2:5).

Currently, we are peacefully coexisting with many unstable nation-states with nuclear weaponry and radical, dictatorial ideologies (ideas). We all know who they are. But, more importantly, there has been no severance of diplomatic relations (communications) with any of these nation-states. In fact, one of them (Russia) tampered with our 2016 Presidential electoral processes. Hence, North Korea would just be one of many, and, therefore, should be dealt with through diplomatic channels as suggested by Secretary of State Tillerson. By any standard, America should not allow an individual who has been referred to as a moron to say to the world-community; dam the torpedoes, full speed ahead to nuclear war.

America, this is not Presidential leadership or patriotism, but a collectivistic death-wish! All Americans should understand ambition and the desire for power. Has President Trump by appointing so many military leaders in his administration created conditions for a military-style coup: banana republic? America might survive, but she will never be the same. It is an obvious fact that America could literally destroy North Korea, but at what cost? And, what have we gained (destroyed)? North Korea is a backward nation that cannot feed itself, and, apparently, populated by the descendants of Cain (killers). America's foundation was built upon the spiritual idea of "I am my brother's keeper." Moreover, America should seek to teach this spiritual-moral truth to North Korea, with or without nuclear weaponry. America, in this Scriptural verse, God is speaking redemption: "If my people, which are called by my name, shall humble themselves, and pray, and seek my face, and turn from their wicked ways; then will I hear from heaven, and will forgive their sin, and will heal their land" (2 Chronicle 7:14). Selah!

Conclusion

When the historical analysis is written and chronicled about the Donald J. Trump Presidency, it shall be recorded as the most divisive, chaotic, spiritually-confused, racist, sexist administration in America's spiritually-troubled-history. To be sure, when President Obama left office the unemployed rate was slightly over 4%. However, in 2008 when Obama assumed the Presidency, the unemployment rate was over 9%. Today, under the Trump Presidency the unemployment rate is at 3.7%. Yet, President Trump is claiming all of the credit for what he calls a great economy. Question: Great for whom, but not all? Thus, Obama's unemployment numbers were "fake-news-reporting" (false) according to Donald J. Trump, but not his numbers. Yet, the numbers are reported by the same reporting agency (source). What a cork-screw-mind!

Donald J. Trump told his loyal supporters that he would build a wall on America's southern border and that Mexico would pay for it. As of yet, no wall has been built and Mexico has said "Hell-No!" But, Trump has militarized the border with federal troops. Walls divide and bridges unite. Lest we forget, President Reagan's, spiritual declaration: "Mr. Gorbachev tear down this wall (Berlin Wall". Of course, no spiritually thoughtful American believed this over-exaggeration anyway. However, Trump's loyal voting base took the bait hook, line, and sinker. President Trump is truly a "GOAT." GOAT is an acronym for: The "Greatness of All Times." Without a doubt, and to be sure, Donald J. Trump owns this title (acronym). He is the greatest Presidential liar of all times. Since assuming the Presidency, Trump has told an average of eight (8) lies a day totaling over 2,000 lies since assuming the Presidency.

It's amazing that the Billy Bush video tape did not sink and derail Donald J. Trump's quest to become President. When a male tells the general public that he is not a "god-fearing-man" you should believe him. For after all, he is telling you not to trust him with the power to govern. Donald J. Trump has emphatically declared that the Mueller investigation is a "Witch Hunt", and that the Russians did not assist his efforts to become President. Yet, his trusted top campaign operatives had relationships with Russians and sought damaging campaign information from Russians.

At the same time, nine Trump campaign officials/operatives have been indicted or pled guilty to crimes against America. Twenty-five Russians have been indicted for seeking to influence the 2016 Presidential election on behalf of Donald J. Trump. And, five Americans have pleaded guilty for their criminality in the 2016 election in exchange for their cooperation in the Mueller investigation. One Russian female operative came to America with the pleasure principle on her mind to subvert "NRA" officials in a criminal "From-Russian-with-a-Love-Sex-Scheme". Their aim was to assist with the election of Donald J. Trump to the Presidency. America, there is an age-old saying "actions speak louder than words," and the actions of the Mueller investigation has captured, ensnared, and produced thirty-five-devilish-witches.

The actions, as expressed in the policy initiatives of President Trump, have primarily been oriented toward re-instituting "white privilege", and the creation and transferring of wealth to those who are already rich. Unfortunately, the election of Barack Obama highlighted the spiritual depth of the racial divide in American society, and Donald J. Trump has become the Drum Major leading the racism parade: "If you are black get back into your place" (The Birther Movement). In 1964-1965 the physical "white-only-signs" were taken down, but for some Whites the signs were written on the heart of their minds, and they cannot "de-whitize" their conscience of racism. Thus, even in the twenty-first century America race still matters in every human interaction, especially in Christian churches where it definitely should not matter at all.

As Christian Americans, we should understand this Scripture verse: "And we know that all things work together for good to them that love God, to them who are the called according to his purpose" (Romans 8:28). A word to the wise is sufficient; therefore, Get right Christian Right Evangelicals, because the Bible has stated it plain and simple: "The Lord gave the word: great was the company of those that published it" (Psalm 68:11). Hence, Republican Party, Christian Right Evangelicals, and Trump Loyalists know this: "Let all things be done decently and in order" (1 Corinthians 14:40). After all, these spiritual lessons should have been taught/learned at home and confirmed in church as a part of everyday living/life; that is: "Lay hands suddenly on no man, neither be a partaker of other men's sins: Keep thyself pure" (1 Timothy 5:22). The Trump Presidency has been an ongoing-nightmare-mistake. Moreover, it has profoundly affected our democratic institutions as well as America's spiritual image in the world community.

The purpose of this book was to socio-spiritually explain using "socio-spiritual-concepts" what has taken place, why it took place, and what will continue to take place as long as Donald J. Trump is President. Americans have become wiser in the Word of God, but spiritually weaker in the flesh (vanity). President Trump has professed himself to be a wise leader. Yet, "Professing themselves to be wise, they became fools" (Romans 1:22). No doubt about it. "And as it is appointed unto men once to die, but after this the judgment" (Hebrew 9:27). America, everyone can take this to his or her grave: "Be not deceived: God is not mocked: for whatsoever a man soweth, that shall he also reap" (Galatians 6:7). Those individuals in the world community, who have a Trumpster mentality, stop the insanity, and madness of your minds to continue to maintain "White-Privilege" for the love of power, money, and sex: PMS. Selah!